CANON DR ROD GARNER is an Anglican priest, writer and theologian, and the author of several books, including *On Being Saved: The roots of redemption* (Darton, Longman and Todd, 2011).

To John.

with best wishes

and fond memories

HOW TO BE WISE

Growing in discernment and love

Rod Garner

First published in Great Britain in 2013

Society for Promoting Christian Knowledge
36 Causton Street
London SW1P 4ST
www.spckpublishing.co.uk

British Library Cataloguing-in-Publication Data
A catalogue record for this book is available from the British Library

ISBN 978–0–281–06893–7
eBook ISBN 978–0–281–06894–4

Typeset by Graphicraft Limited, Hong Kong
First printed in Great Britain by Ashford Colour Press
Subsequently digitally printed in Great Britain

eBook by Graphicraft Limited, Hong Kong

Produced on paper from sustainable forests

For Canon John Gaine:
wise teacher, mentor and friend.
With gratitude and affection.

Contents

Introduction

This is a small book on a huge subject. As I hope to show later, wisdom is not difficult to recognize despite its various guises. Sometimes we just feel its presence or benefit from its judgements. Defining this ancient virtue, however, from its beginnings in the centuries before Christ is a more daunting prospect. I'm also conscious of an understandable pressure to say too much for the sake of comprehensiveness and run the risk of losing you in the detail as an unintended consequence. This is neither my aim nor my intention.

In order to avoid this danger I have kept at the back of my mind some pertinent advice from my academic tutor when I began studying for an external philosophy degree through the University of London some four years into my ministry. He was a fine priest and scholar blessed with intellectual and practical gifts and a study containing hundreds of books piled precariously to the ceiling. I was convinced that at some point before the Day of Judgement, everything would fall down as we debated, but it never did. During one of our earliest tutorials he introduced me to the world of formal logic – a demanding and tiring session but one that ended amicably. We said goodbye, only for me then to discover that my car would not start. Slipping on a pair of overalls, this man of considerable learning disappeared under the bonnet and resurrected the engine! His declared preference, he once told me, was for 'small books on big themes rather than the opposite'. Even then I think I understood. Relatively few have the patience, time or inclination to wade through tomes, however worthy, so I've opted for brevity and tried to avoid the crass or superficial. In this important matter, you will, of course, be the final judge!

In terms of value, let me tell you briefly what you can expect from this purchase. You will not find a rough guide for the perplexed between these covers, still less one of those seductive, best-selling manuals of instruction that guarantee weight loss, well-being or, in this case, wisdom with a minimum of discomfort in 30 days or your money back! I've set my sights a little higher. What I want to share with you are insights and stories, epiphanies and journeys, encounters and experiences that have for me proved instructive and sometimes remarkable.

I have another ambition, and that is to convince you of the importance of questions as a means of seeking wisdom. I believe in questions almost as much as I believe in those other timeless and lovely things – truth and beauty – and you are about to discover lots of them bubbling under the surface of this book. They represent questions of a particular kind: the sort that prompt wonder, that occasionally keep us awake at night or even require us to re-evaluate our lives and priorities. I hope to persuade you that questions are frequently more satisfying than the bland or unconvincing answers that religion is prone to give when life becomes muddled or lets us down. A question can contain a great religious truth and help us to love God with our minds as well as our hearts.

There is a fair bit of me in what follows – some of it quite personal. Exploring the significance of the human emotions at the precise time my mother's life was drawing to its end proved both moving and illuminating in a way that I could not have anticipated. Similarly, the concluding reflections on silence led me down unexpected byways that had in no way figured in my early drafting of that chapter.

Voices other than mine, you will be glad to hear, are ready to address you in the wings. Theologians and philosophers, writers and composers, poets and saints all await your attention and response. I have been in conversation with them for some considerable time. They have enriched my life and kept me on the road to what the poet William Blake called 'the palace of wisdom'. The Bible also figures prominently. In writing these chapters, I have been able to grapple with three scriptural authors of immense significance. Their wisdom – so much deeper than our own in relation to our time on earth, what we should do with it, and how we should look at Jesus in a way that might actually change us – questions our own frequently lazy assumptions and invites us to reflect again on 'things of good report' (Phil. 4.8).

The one thing I know for certain concerning wisdom is that it represents a lifetime's endeavour, and that for me is part of its attraction. It demands the best of us in the pursuit of what one great nineteenth-century social reformer described in another context as 'deep, difficult, holy work'; it is, I think, best understood, rather like theology itself, as a standpoint or perspective informed by prayer and silence and sustained reflection on how things seem to be in the world. Currently, and I suspect for some years yet, we are going to remain in the centre of what the writer and commentator Francis Fukuyama has described as the Great Disruption. Not even the best-informed observers of our social, economic and moral upheaval can tell us where this will lead or how it will end. In the painful and unsettling interim, however, wisdom can teach us patience and encourage us in the practice of compassion. Staying human, particularly in what is for many a dark time, feels to me like an eleventh commandment for an unsettling age. Wisdom has a significant role to play in how well and how faithfully we respond.

Some acknowledgements are in order. This book began its life in New York. There I benefited from conversations with writers and musicians, priests and theologians, and lay members of the Episcopalian Church who repeatedly displayed an impressive talent for ideas and issues at 8.30 each morning over coffee! I wish to thank them and the Diocese of Liverpool for helping to make such an enjoyable and stimulating visit possible. In the space of little more than a month I encountered individuals from different parts of America and the global Anglican Church.

I led worship, welcomed those who had come to meditate and spoke frequently to receptive gatherings. I also learned much from unplanned encounters and the courtesy of strangers. All this was shared with Christine, and for this too, thanks.

Rod Garner
Feast of the Presentation of Christ in the Temple

1

What is wisdom?

A book on wisdom almost demands that it should begin with something profound – the musings of a mystic, for example, or the dazzling insights of a sacred text. I'm keeping these for later and opting instead for the element of surprise. My first witness, so to speak, is neither philosopher nor scholar in a professional sense but a comedian and film-maker with the endearing ability to treat serious questions in a light-hearted way.

Now in his eighth decade, Woody Allen remains a prolific artist producing work to critical acclaim. A generation ago he was the poster boy of box-office cinema, mining a rich and hilarious vein of comedy from closely observed lives that he portrayed with a keen but kindly eye. He enlightened as well as entertained, and along with receptive audiences I found myself drawn to his vulnerability, humour and restlessness. Forever questioning and obsessing about relationships, religion and the strange ways of the world, he mirrored some of our own concerns and, to our relief, found them equally perplexing. A refreshing sense of the ridiculous also tempered his quips and observations on the nature of reality. Two stay in my mind: 'If everything is illusion and nothing is real, I've definitely paid too much for my carpet.' The other, concerning the end of life (and rather better known), led him to the conclusion that he wasn't frightened by death, he just didn't want to be around when it happened. None of us is around for our death, of course; as the philosopher Wittgenstein pointed out, death is not an event in life, we just mistake it for dying – a quite different thing.

1

In one of his finest films, *Hannah and her Sisters* (1986), Allen's character, prompted by an acute sense of his own mortality, consults a slew of gurus, psychiatrists and clerics in the hope of staving off his morbid anxieties. He tries to follow their guidance and instructions but nothing works. Seeking relief from his misery, he goes to the movies and unexpectedly finds an answer of sorts to his dilemmas in the cheerful closing scenes of the Marx Brothers' film *Duck Soup*. He consoles himself with the thought that even if life is brief and baffling and too often short on epiphanies, we can still, like the characters in the film he has been watching, laugh and sing along the way and try to worry less. This strikes him as a serendipitous form of wisdom – a way of coping with uncertainties as we count our days and gaze into an uncharted future that rarely conforms to programmed hopes or expectations.

Even if we disagree with Allen's conclusion, the film reminds us that the search for wisdom, in whatever form, retains its hold on us. I'm writing these words in New York City while on a month-long assignment for the Episcopal Church. Here clairvoyants and tarot card readers occupy the personal columns of newspapers and magazines. The self-help literature of secular gurus fills the shelves of major book stores and Oprah Winfrey is finally bowing out from a show that has made her a billionaire and given her an immensely powerful platform to convey her beliefs in psychics, angels and a variety of spiritual alternatives to conventional religion. She has presided over a huge audience, and because she believed, millions of others did too. In austere or dangerous times we want to be wise when the ground shifts beneath our feet or financial institutions stagger. And we need wisdom not only to make some sense of the unexpected, cruel and absurd but also to lead meaningful lives before, in the words of Psalm 90, we 'are soon gone, and we fly away'. Wisdom holds no promise of a secure happiness but it can help us to ask the right questions, think differently and recognize the claims of others on our lives in a globalized but increasingly polarized world.

In the early 1960s, Marshall McLuhan coined the term 'global village' as the new medium of television held out a vista of human solidarity. The early promise he spoke of has still to be fulfilled. In some respects we are closer, but we also inhabit a more ephemeral and tenuous world. Remarkable advances in technology have made communication easier, but without always bringing us together. Frequently, the world does not feel like a village and social networks can leave users feeling vulnerable or lost.[1] As the celebrated Polish foreign correspondent Ryszard Kapuscinski reminds us: 'the essence of a village depends on the fact that its inhabitants know each other well, commune with each other and share a common fate'.[2]

If knowing what wisdom can do for us is one thing, defining it is another. Inevitably, perhaps, there is no shortage of disagreement, particularly within the academy. In an anthology published in 1990 entitled *Wisdom: Its Nature, Origins and Development*, 13 notable thinkers each offered a different interpretation.[3] It would appear that in order to grasp wisdom in its most comprehensive sense, more wisdom is required than any one person can muster! On the one hand it is one of our most valued aspirations, on the other, one of the least understood and most elusive. None of this requires us to fall silent though, as most of us have an intuitive sense of what wisdom means or looks like. It conjures images of dreaming spires and faces deep in thought and invites us to view luminaries such as Socrates, Jesus or the Buddha as worthy of emulation.

Beyond such images, however, when we actually start to think about wisdom a mental fog can emerge. Depending on our perspective and beliefs, it can be a divine attribute, a human endeavour or a partnership that unites heaven and earth. Wisdom straddles several disciplines – historically, and most obviously, philosophy but also theology, psychology, sociology and political science. The inclusion of political science will puzzle some, given the continuing low standing of politics and politicians, but no less an authority than Aristotle insisted that the human activity that most adequately addresses 'what people shall do and refrain from doing' for the sake of the wider community is political science. Any investigation into the ethics and ends of any action, therefore, 'is in a sense the study of politics'.[4] Literature and poetry complete wisdom's armoury, as for many, including myself, they represent trusted sources of truth.

We face a paradox here: to be truly wise is to acknowledge how little we know and how ignorant we often are concerning the best that has been thought and taught. We also lack the time for what venerable Greek thinkers such as Aristotle describe as 'the examined life' – for them the only life worth living and the means whereby actions and problems are seen in a different light in order that we might become morally rounded individuals. From my reading and observations, however, I remain convinced that this high ambition still endures, despite the many demands (real or imagined) that erode our days. The good life that has at its heart the aim of a practical wisdom that shapes our moral identity retains its appeal, particularly when so much of the moral landscape seems fuzzy and the white noise of the information age invites us to know everything, except what is worth knowing.[5]

Note that word 'practical'. The pursuit of wisdom is not a pointless exercise in abstractions that seeks to bind the truth with ropes of sand. It delivers by holding the key to 'moral clarity'[6] – the clear-sightedness that exposes moral deficiencies of action or intent (whether personal or political) and helps to shape our desires and ambitions to better ends. In a 1987 essay entitled 'What is Wisdom and Why do Philosophers Love it So?', the philosopher Robert Nozick answers his own question succinctly in the opening paragraph: 'Wisdom is an understanding of what is important, where this understanding informs a (wise) person's thoughts or actions.'[7] The reply seems straightforward enough, but it masks two issues that I shall come to shortly. It does, however, confirm my earlier point that wisdom moves things on and makes demands on us. It requires us to focus and reflect, to discard a piece of knowledge, rule or habit when it is no longer true or useful and to set our personal goals against those wider human needs and longings that we continue to describe, with no irony intended, as 'the common good'.[8]

Even to think about wisdom, to allow ourselves the mental space to consider what being wise in any given situation might amount to, brings us closer to the thing itself. Researching the philosophical roots of wisdom, the science writer Stephen Hall concludes:

> Simply put, thinking about wisdom forces you to think about the way you lead your life, just as reading about wisdom, I believe, forces you to wrestle with its meanings and implications. You might come to think of this exercise, as I have, as an enlightened form of self-consciousness, almost an armchair form of mindfulness or meditation that cannot help but inform our actions. And that's another key point: to separate wisdom from action is a form of malpractice in the conduct of one's life. 'We ought to seek out virtue not merely to contemplate it,' Plutarch wrote, 'but to derive benefit from doing so'.[9]

Science and philosophy agree at this point: wisdom concerns itself with what is good, and can benefit everyone provided it does not become an indulgent form of introspection. We are making some progress, and in order to make further headway through the fog I want to return to Nozick's earlier definition. First, although he is right to emphasize the importance of informed and practical choices, wisdom is not just about decision-making, however ethical or admirable. Neither is it a set of facts or values, an exclusive body of knowledge or a specific kind of moral expertise. It looks and feels more akin to the attitude and disposition we display towards a whole range of things, including our deepest beliefs and assumptions. And it's also about the patience and humility that tell us we frequently get things wrong and the compassion that is prepared to stand in the shoes of another. In one sense it's also true that we know wisdom when we see it without necessarily being able to explain it. Asked to choose in terms of importance between the medical researcher who devotes her life to finding a cure for rare childhood cancers and the local real ale enthusiast who spends every waking hour amassing the world's largest collection of decorative beer mats, we can be fairly certain who will get our vote. We just know.

My second concern is that Nozick seems to reduce wisdom to an autonomous human quality or virtue. It is indeed that – tutored moral sense calls for a lot of hard thought and sound judgement on our part – but in telling right from wrong and truth from falsehood, in constructing the relationships that build trust and extend respect towards all things, many people (not infrequently religious or given to serious reflection) look to texts and individuals beyond their own immediate experience as sources of wisdom. Not, we must add, as a means of using such information uncritically or harmfully: fundamentalism in all its modern manifestations is an affront to true wisdom. In this respect it's worth remembering that it was the power of a warped and morally repugnant idea that led a handful of terrorists to change for ever the skyline of New York on 11 September 2001. By contrast, it's important and reassuring to note how our capacity for moral reasoning and wise decisions can be strengthened through our acquaintance with the telling or revelatory experiences enshrined in a story, a proverb, a gospel or a creed.

While in New York, my wife Christine and I visited the Park Avenue synagogue, a prominent centre of Reformed Judaism there with an impressive department of adult education that aims to foster experiences of Jewish life and inter-faith dialogue. The current programme runs to 29 pages, taking in everything from home learning, book discussion groups, social action and cemetery conservation to lectures and visits from distinguished speakers and scholars. In the library, synagogue members can learn Torah, read novels, surf the Web, chat in Yiddish or (in the case of younger worshippers) play with Hebrew alphabet blocks! We were given a gracious reception and the freedom to walk around the building unhindered by staff or the security guard. The walls display many references to the Holocaust, but it was a painting far removed from the death camps of the twentieth century that detained me more than the rest.

Let me try to describe it for you. Entitled *Torah*, it is a vivid and passionate depiction of a synagogue interior from an earlier age. An old and bearded rabbi commands the centre of attention. He exudes a formidable physical presence but it is the large scroll in his hands that captivates the male worshippers in front of him. Some reach out in the hope of touching the scroll, others look on awestruck while those in the background avidly read their prayer books. The painting conveys a richly evocative image of the talismanic power of the Torah and the profound, almost visceral relationship between the pious assembly and the laws that lend the deepest wisdom to their lives. Even a sceptic, I suspect, would find this scene impressive. Here we see a congregation rooted and grounded in laws evoked by a particular story and elaborated in a sacred book. They are wedded to Torah and palpably draw strength and inspiration from its wisdom. They are indebted to a scripture that mediates their history and suffering and represents the genesis of their continuing human story as the covenantal people of the Most High.

Historically, other stories have generated the same awe and insights. In 2009, in the House of the Redeemer, a retreat house of the Episcopal Church in New York, a group of professional story-tellers presented the epic narrative of Gilgamesh, considered to be one of the masterpieces of world literature. Gilgamesh is civilization's first story – a thousand years older than the Iliad or the Bible. The 11 tablets on which the story was written were found in the ruins of Nineveh, in present-day Iraq. They tell of the historical king who reigned in the Mesopotamian city of Uruk in about 2750 BC and his journey of self-discovery. On his travels Gilgamesh discerns that friendship can bring peace to an entire city, that a pre-emptive attack on a monster can have distressing consequences, and that wisdom can be found only when the quest for it is abandoned. Like the most rewarding and tantalizing stories in Scripture, the wisdom of Gilgamesh rests on its moral insights, metaphors, poetry and paradoxes that can be interpreted as forms of poetic truth or divine inspiration, which are offered as gifts to the reader, especially the initiated.

We can see the same principle at work elsewhere in the great world religions. The Qur'an, for example, is venerated by Islam as a form of holy dictation initially disclosed to the prophet Muhammad over 23 years from AD 610. During that period it was memorized, recited and precisely written down by Muhammad's companions after each revelation, eventually forming a compendium of moral and spiritual guidance and specific historical events. The extraordinary collection of Indian writings known as the Upanishads that are central to Hinduism contain for their adherents the fundamental truths of the universe. One of the oldest and longest texts, the Brihadaranyaka, offers a way of liberation that leads 'from the unreal to the real, from darkness to light, from death to immortality'. It calls for a spiritual awakening on the part of humanity and warns the reader that there must be an increase in wisdom as well as knowledge if the latter is to promote our flourishing. For some of the greatest Indian mystics and spiritual leaders, the Upanishads were held to have no beginning in time and were venerated as messages from another world of purity and undivided truth.[10]

Buddhism, by contrast, has its genesis in the life of Prince Siddhartha. Around 530 BC, shortly before his thirtieth birthday, he renounced a life of ease and luxury and retreated into a forest. There he sat under a Bodhi tree until he received the enlightenment that led to the stilling of all desire and the enunciation of the Four Noble Truths that came to represent for him

the art of living and dying.[11] For 45 years he wandered throughout East India offering a gospel of 'complete attentiveness' and
a personal striving towards selflessness. Anticipating another,
later teacher who taught by the Sea of Galilee and journeyed
through the towns and villages of Palestine, the Prince wrote
none of his teachings down, but they were safeguarded by the
corporate recitations of his disciples.

Preserved in the first instance by oral tradition, they were
eventually transcribed on to birch bark by monks in Sri Lanka
around AD 17. They remain a treasured repository of wisdom,
and we have on record the accounts of Buddhist holy men who
were prepared to sacrifice everything in their attempts to safe-
guard and discover the definitive texts of their guru. In AD 399,
Chinese monk Fa Hsien resolved to reach India overland from
the valley of the Yellow River. He negotiated high mountains and
treacherous roads before crossing a desert 'of evil demons and
hot winds' to a land 'where snow rests winter and summer,
and there are dragons which spit wind'. More than 200 years
later, a similar route was pursued by another monk, Hsuan
Tsang. His scribe Hui-li records that his master desired one
thing only, far above wealth or fame: religious truth. Tsang
almost died on the journey. The endless sand offered no hospitality, there was no trace of man or beast and at night 'demons
and goblins raised fire-lights to confound the stars'. He eventually entered India over the Hindu Kush and spent two years of
spiritual preparation in Kashmir before 'following the course
of the Ganges from monastery to monastery'.[12]

This tenacious and extraordinary commitment to Buddhist
wisdom, shot through with danger and romance, is no fairy tale
and finds a contemporary resonance in the life of Gene Smith,
Tibetologist and librarian. In the early 1960s Smith went to India
as a student seeking rare Tibetan books. This was just a few years
after Tibet's 1959 uprising against the Chinese occupiers, when
the country's monasteries were vandalized and destroyed. Sacred
books were burned, along with the carved wooden blocks from

which they were printed; 1,500 years of thought and prayerful reflection were torched. Faithful Tibetans tried to preserve some of the texts as they fled, tying them on yaks or even their own backs, but much was lost as precious loads fell into rivers and ravines. Over the course of 50 years, Smith as librarian and Buddhist resolved to put the literature back together again. His life was spent in rigorous discipline among the ancient texts on which he believed spiritual progress depended.

He found two ways to save books, both ingenious. Armed with cash carved out of an American food-aid programme that made provision for local humanitarian ventures, he spent 20 years in India travelling into the hills. There his patent devotion endeared him to exiled Tibetan monks, still fearful of revealing their treasures. He won their confidence and they showed him their texts. The money he gave them enabled them to print more copies. His conservation programme saved 8,000 books, and 20 copies of each were produced for research centres in the USA.

In 1999 he established the Tibetan Buddhist Resource Centre, initially in Boston, later transferring to New York, where his 12,000-volume collection was placed online. Before his death in December 2010 he and his colleagues had scanned 7 million pages of text, and made CDs of other Buddhist teaching that would simply take too long to download. On his spiritual travels he would hand out devices no bigger than the palm of a hand containing 10,000 books. Monks who were used to reading loose leaves on their knees could now stare into laptops, contemplating the works Smith had scanned for them. In 2008, at the monastery of Menri in the foothills of the Himalayas, he presented the abbot with a memory stick and asked him to wear it as an amulet around his neck. The abbot wears it with his crimson robes – a portable and precious repository of hundreds of pages of scriptures that could so easily have perished. In Smith's hands, the memory stick became the modern incarnation of *terma* – tiny texts of former Buddhist times contained in shell-like casings, which were buried in the ground and were intended to be dug up again at some future date in the hope of speaking wisdom to later generations.[13]

All the above examples find parallels in Christianity, both in terms of the veneration of sacred texts and the extent to which the generations after Jesus took upon themselves the task of conserving what had been handed on to them. The New Testament itself makes no sense unless it is understood as a concerted attempt to communicate the words and voice of a unique teacher, who was followed and then worshipped as the supreme oracle of God. As a 'people of the Book' we are also indebted to the Church for the wisdom that has been declared to us in Christ. It is the Church that has ensured that the texts we esteem have not been denied their inspired status or relegated to the level of fables. For the greater part of Christian history, the teaching office of the Church has safeguarded the shape, content and integrity of Christian believing.

In particular, the formative centuries of Christianity bear witness to the strange and eccentric doctrines that surfaced in the name of Christ and the robust response of orthodoxy to such claims.[14] Mistakes, hurts and fatalities characterized the great doctrinal controversies, and later centuries provided ample evidence of a worrying tendency on the part of ecclesiastical authority to suppress or condemn deep, honest intellectual thought, even within the Church. In 1864, Pius IX, the first Pope empowered by the Church to make infallible statements on its behalf, ruled that Catholics could no longer have liberal thoughts or engage with a secular and threatening culture allegedly mired in errors.[15] All this is far from the mind of Christ who came to set us free. But even as we acknowledge the sporadic ecclesiastical blindness and hardness of heart that have dishonoured his name, a generous measure of respect can be given to a Church that, in the face of hostility and intellectual contempt that continue to this day,[16] still venerates the teachings of Christ as its own, for the sake of all who would be truly wise in this generation and the next.

11

To recap: we have located sources of wisdom in the existential choices we make as reflective persons, the stories, texts and creeds we live by and the authority of religious institutions when they genuinely seek and teach divine truths. We have also encountered a number of wise men who without the benefit of a guiding star gave birth to upheavals of thought. In turn, their dedicated followers made great sacrifices to act as 'mail carriers'[17] for the truths they believed had been entrusted to them. I propose to add one more to their number and shortly I shall explain the reason for his inclusion.

Even up to a week before writing this chapter, I was not certain about my prospective choice: other pre-eminent persons cluttered my mind and the demon of procrastination was beginning to torment! A leisurely walk through Madison Square Park on a magnificent afternoon dissolved all my hesitations. Initially, my attention was seized by an open-top parade celebrating the fifth anniversary of a pulsating New York disco. The music was loud yet irresistibly infectious. On the top of the bus, the cheerleaders – young women with little by way of clothing to impede their movements – danced to the beat and waved to the growing and varied band of appreciative onlookers. Behind them followed scores of people, hands in the air, gyrating as they moved with all the easy grace of youth. Kindness pervaded everything. It looked and felt like a cavalcade of hope – both a celebration of a recent and lively musical past and the present moment and an intimation of future promise. Part of me wanted to join in but an Anglican temperament and an ageing body proved powerful disqualifiers in a hip-hop procession! Nevertheless, I was still caught up with the energy and beauty of it all, so much so that I almost failed to see a statue some 25 yards away in the Park. Christine noticed it first and quickly pointed me to the image of a small, bald man inclining slightly forward, with only a staff, his trademark loin-cloth and steel-rimmed glasses by way of adornment. Quite probably you have already deduced his identity from this description. If not, I'm speaking here of Mohandas K. Gandhi, and for two reasons.

Gandhi is remembered and venerated as a religious and social reformer (hence the title of Mahatma), a leader in the Indian nationalist movement of the last century and a powerful advocate of non-violent civil resistance. Many have been inspired by his writings, not least in the American civil rights campaigns, and in India he remains a national icon – a touchstone by which private and public standards of morality continue to be judged. But he was also a lover of wisdom who viewed the authentic human life as a search for God, or truth, manifested in peaceful action, self-discipline and service to humanity. He wrote prolifically and read extensively and in his search for wisdom he came to realize that all religious traditions had some spiritual and ethical value. Like Augustine before him, he was not easily drawn to the Old Testament and confessed to falling asleep as he wrestled with its more baffling texts. By contrast the New Testament touched him profoundly, along with the Hindu scriptural text the Bhagavad Gita. The writings of Leo Tolstoy had a similar effect, and a little book by the British author John Ruskin, *Unto this Last*, led to deep changes in his personal way of life.[18] He was also influenced by Muslim and Christian friends, and would sometimes quote the line 'one step enough for me' from Cardinal Newman's great Victorian hymn, 'Lead, kindly Light'. He would probably have come across the hymn while he was in London; he arrived in 1888, aged just 18, full of fear and trembling but with a fierce desire to make a new life.

From humble beginnings (Gandhi means 'grocer' in Gujarati) and impaired by fragile health and crippling shyness, he began studying law. He stood out for the wrong reasons: a vegetarian, dressed in strange, unsuitable clothes in a city of marked social distinctions, where the image of the English gentleman was assiduously cultivated by his more affluent contemporaries. By his own admission and the simple fact of his birth, gentlemanly

He came
to Bajworth
:- 1912

aspirations were beyond him; for the sake of a concerned English friend, however, he attempted to become a follower of fashion. He acquired a top hat, a silk shirt and bold tie, a double-breasted waistcoat, striped trousers and patent leather shoes complete with spats. Gloves and a silver cane completed this new look, and to further his credentials even more he bought a violin, studied elocution and enrolled for dancing lessons. The makeover and the attempts at cultural refinement lasted about three months. There was no vanity in either endeavour. Gandhi simply wanted to repay the kindness of his friend and to find out whether such gestures might ease him into polite society. They didn't, and at that point his fashion ambitions ceased. At a very young age Gandhi displayed a wisdom and self-awareness that remain instructive. Possessed of a humility that had no wish to offend needlessly, he was also ready when necessary to forfeit his illusions and pretensions in order to reinstate the deeper habits of his heart.

Much later in life, the nascent self-awareness of his late adolescence matured into a remarkable strength. His faltering speech taught him the economy of words and his ability to order his needs and desires liberated his most important energies for the non-violent mass political movement we associate with his name. First as a young lawyer in South Africa, and then in the bloody and prolonged fight for Indian independence, he drew on the teachings of the Upanishads and the Buddha and sought to empty himself of all the vain things that frequently thwart our more worthy intuitions. When confronted with intimidation and physical abuse, he refused to back down and with an unyielding commitment to social justice he spoke truth to power. This small, frail man insisted that he would be heard as he challenged authority on behalf of the powerless. His limitations proved no impediment to his cause and his innate humility fostered the wisdom that wedded his deep moral sense to the duty of resistance.

By his deeds, Gandhi demonstrated the correlation between humility and wisdom – a link well documented in philosophy.

Immanuel Kant regarded humility as one of the essential virtues – the means whereby we know ourselves to be only human with the talent to deceive (and sometimes destroy) but also capable of decent, dignified and rational acts. In this respect, the lesser term 'humble' doesn't even begin to contain the measure of humility in its strongest sense. Gandhi was not humble, nor was Jesus, and neither made the mistake of equating humility with mere obedience and submission to superiors. Uncommonly focused in terms of their aims, and ready when necessary to challenge or reprimand, they were nevertheless able to stand back and think again in the light of another's questions or needs. Gandhi transformed his attire for a while; and Jesus, after crossing the Sea of Galilee, rescheduled his itinerary in the face of reported suffering despite the clamour of the crowd pressing in on him (Mark 5.21–24). More remarkably still, to me, he changed his mind when a Gentile woman insisted on the moral propriety of her cause. Initially ignored by Jesus, who then urged his disciples to send her away, she stood her ground and reminded him that her plea was just. We register the heartbreak and resoluteness in her voice before we hear the gracious acknowledgement of her faith and the granting of her request (Matt. 15.21–28). Few people are wise enough to prefer criticism or questioning to praise, but humility makes such wisdom possible. In the scene I've just described, moral clarity was made possible by a conversation between two self-confident characters who knew when to stand firm but also when to yield.

The Gentile woman has still more to teach us, for she reminds us that wisdom is not the exclusive preserve of wise men, whether from the East or any other sphere. Stephen Hall comments helpfully:

> Wisdom clearly isn't a trait conferred by a gene sequestered on the male Y chromosome. For every Solomon there is a Sarah and an Esther; for every Pericles, there is his little-known

mistress Aspasia, who, according to Plutarch, was one of the wisest people in that wisest era of Greek civilisation. For every Jesus, a Mary Magdalene; for every Mandela an Aung San Suu Kyi. In the Bible, wisdom is a She.[19]

I could stop here, as this last quotation provides the perfect link to the next chapter. But I have one more passage to share that reinforces the point made much earlier – the difficulty of reducing wisdom to a simple formula or definition,[20] and discerning (before we even get to practising them) the virtues that help to make us wise. It's part of a book review worth pondering before we turn to the wisdom literature of the Hebrew Bible:

> As far back as I can remember, my father encouraged me to read one chapter of the book of Proverbs every day for an entire month: thirty-one days (for most months) and thirty-one chapters – not an onerous task even for the most infrequent reader. The habit, with more or less regularity, stuck with me. In the course of studying such penetrating, comforting, and immensely practical words, I found myself frustrated by the paradoxical nature of it all. No matter how diligently one pursues wisdom – even attains it – he or she can never admit that they 'got it' . . . Wisdom is a fool's quest but only a fool would ignore the importance of pursuing it . . .[21]

Wisdom, it seems, is our care, our duty and, sometimes, even our delight.

2

The Hebrew Scriptures and the wisdom of Ecclesiastes

An integral and important part of my life as a priest is to conduct funerals. Some months – and not necessarily the darkest or coldest – the local crematorium seems like my second home. There, in a modest chapel, with congregations sometimes small and sometimes overflowing its doors, I attempt to speak a word of hope and encouragement to grieving assemblies. I commend souls to God, give comfort to the bereaved and remind everyone that we are caught in the web of time and there is wisdom to be had in living well the days left to us here on earth. I use music, prayer and the quietness that fittingly attends the ache of the human heart confronted by loss. And I try to find the best words for the occasion: poetry, prose, the New Testament – in fact, anything that has informed my understanding of this perplexing continuum we call life and the even greater mystery of the hush of death.

Increasingly, in recent years I've found myself turning to the book of Ecclesiastes as the right text to mark this final rite of passage. In particular, the first eight verses of Chapter 3:

> For everything there is a season, and a time for every
>   matter under heaven:
> a time to be born, and a time to die;
> a time to plant, and a time to pluck up what is planted;
> a time to kill, and a time to heal;
> a time to break down, and a time to build up;
> a time to weep, and a time to laugh;
> a time to mourn, and a time to dance;

> a time to throw away stones, and a time to gather stones together;
> a time to embrace, and a time to refrain from embracing;
> a time to seek, and a time to lose;
> a time to keep, and a time to throw away;
> a time to tear, and a time to sew;
> a time to keep silence, and a time to speak;
> a time to love, and a time to hate;
> a time for war, and a time for peace.

I can never be quite sure what the mourners make of these verses or even if they know where they are from – Shakespeare, a pop song from the 1960s, a love sonnet to loss – but frequently the words seem to connect. Listeners in the main will have little grasp of the Bible – Ecclesiastes? Who's he? But they do appear engaged by this profound and deeply poetic meditation on transience, with its repetitive rhythms and its sense of life as a fragile and extraordinary gift. 'For everything there is a season . . . a time to be born, and a time to die.' There is no false piety here or religious platitudes drained of power by endless repetition. Rather, we hear the voice of Qoheleth, the preacher and teacher identified in the opening verse of the book:[1] a voice that is in turn elegant, gloomy, sceptical and strangely reassuring, as in successive chapters it speaks with startling economy of human desires, wasted ambitions and the importance of the fleeting moment when 'light is sweet, and it is pleasant for the eyes to see the sun' (Eccles. 11.7). It is also a dispassionate voice revealing a definite and highly idiosyncratic personality and a take on life replete with the questions and conclusions of a wise man pondering what humans can expect in an ambiguous world.

For all its distinctiveness, however, this is a voice with antecedents and parallels in Old Testament conceptions of wisdom that are to be found elsewhere in Proverbs, Job, Sirach and the Wisdom of Solomon.[2] If in one sense Ecclesiastes stands alone in its range of concerns and its unflinching realism concerning the haphazard jumble that is the world, we must also locate its voice within a wider tradition of Hebrew enquiry, precepts and cultivated knowledge that with awe, patience and diffidence sought out 'the steep path of wisdom'.[3] We need to know something about this in order to appreciate fully the surprising and novel insights of Ecclesiastes and the extent to which they afford to wisdom a new name.

Where to begin? Perhaps with the realization that for ancient Israel, the concept of wisdom is variously subtle, complex, questioning, didactic, paradoxical and occasionally dark. It is concerned with both the cultivation of moral virtues, especially the righteousness and truth that flow from keeping the commandments and fearing God, and the duty to expose the human foolishness, excess and stubbornness that frequently call for correction and blind us to the true nature of things and how we are to relate to them. Wisdom emphasizes the importance of health, honesty and hospitality, the duty of honouring parents, marriage and children, the use and abuse of riches, the observance of religious duties and our obligations to neighbours, friends and strangers.[4] And it does not shrink from the prescriptive. Here are just a few examples, accompanied by their modern counterparts:

'Keep your tongue from evil and your lips from speaking deceit' (Ps. 34.13): Do not lie.

'Those with good sense are slow to anger, and it is their glory to overlook an offence' (Prov. 19.11): Be patient.

'A person's pride will bring humiliation, but one who is lowly in spirit will obtain honour' (Prov. 29.23): Humility is the proper disposition of the righteous person.

'Death and life are in the power of the tongue' (Prov. 18.21): The necessity of self-control.

'The beginning of strife is like letting out water; so stop before the quarrel breaks out' (Prov. 17.14): Peace and reconciliation is encouraged.

'Do not be among winebibbers, or among gluttonous eaters of meat; for the drunkard and the glutton will come to poverty' (Prov. 23.20–21): Temperance in matters of food and drink is a necessary thing.[5]

In such precepts lie the possibilities of a righteous life and the creation of a good society. In this respect, wisdom has an instrumental thrust: it seeks the proper ordering of human desires and the fostering of obligations that look beyond the individual to the well-being of the wider community.[6] It has, in addition, an educative purpose. It teaches the importance of the past (Job 15.4–8) and hands on received traditions, often tempered with fresh insights (Prov. 15.2, 7; Eccles. 12.9). The wise person knows that our understanding is partial and that learning is increased by drawing on the experiences of others (Prov. 1.8). Learning is life-long because the work of wisdom is never done. The foolish are always slow to recognize this; then, as now in a computerized, electronic age, they presume that wisdom is just one more commodity to be acquired along with others: 'Why should fools have a price in hand to buy wisdom, when they have no mind to learn?' (Prov. 17.16). Wisdom is not a product bought over the counter or available instantly and effortlessly at the touch of a button. It takes time, draws on the past, embraces the shared understandings of the community, and in humility concedes its limitations set against the inscrutable reality of God:

> Trust in the LORD with all your heart,
>   and do not rely on your own insight.
> In all your ways acknowledge him,
>   and he will make straight your paths.
>   (Prov. 3.5–6)

We note the paradox: wisdom is a work that demands the best of us. But whenever its pursuit leads to a false sense of security or boasting in our own achievements, 'wisdom has already cancelled itself out'.[7]

Another paradox to confront us concerns what is best described as a clash of world-views. In Proverbs there is a golden thread of optimism predicated on the belief that obedience and faith, combined with a healthy regard for the divine will that orders all things, bring blessing and fortune in their train: the one who toils shall never want for bread (12.19; 28.11); the home is safe in the hands of the good wife who 'is not afraid ... and looks well to the ways of her household' (31.21, 27); and the righteous are delivered from trouble (11.8). Conversely, the wicked and rapacious will have their reward in the form of a bitter harvest and when they die 'their hope perishes' (11.7). A reassuring picture emerges of a moral universe in which rewards and punishments are meted out accordingly. This, however, is not the world we actually know, where frequently honest labourers perish through lack of bread and wickedness often carries the day. A world where fairness seems in short supply and wealth accumulates even more wealth and the poor remain downtrodden.

Such brute facts do not go unacknowledged elsewhere in the wisdom literature. The book of Job may be seen as an extended protest against unwarranted optimism and a tendency in Proverbs to disregard tragedy and calamities. Reflecting on Job, the great Danish theologian and philosopher Søren Kierkegaard notes:

> And yet there is no hiding place in the wide world where troubles may not find you, and there has never lived a man who was able to say more than you can say, that you do not know when sorrow will visit your house. So be sincere with yourself, fix your eyes upon Job; even though he terrifies you, it is not this he wishes, if you yourself do not wish it.[8]

Elsewhere, in the Wisdom of Solomon and, as we shall see shortly, in Ecclesiastes, there can also be found darker, more pessimistic conclusions that reflect disillusionment with life in general and disappointment or resignation that, notwithstanding the virtues of the honest and upright and the misdemeanours of wrongdoers, ultimately the same fate awaits them all: 'We were born by mere chance and hereafter we shall be as though we had never been' (Wisd. 2.2). A gloomy prognosis for sure, and a world removed from the sunny certainties of Proverbs.

How can we account for these different perspectives? Context is a big factor. Most scholars agree that the wisdom literature of ancient Israel was influenced by Egyptian and Sumarian forerunners. Both types of wisdom, providential and sceptical, were appropriated by the Hebrews: the former in Proverbs, and the darker search for divine justice in Job and Ecclesiastes. In other words, Jewish ideas became interwoven with non-Jewish world-views – the Wisdom of Solomon, for example, conveying a time of unease or disquiet, 'perhaps reflecting Roman rule in Egypt, and the influence of Hellenistic values in the first century BC'.[9] Wisdom speaks with more than one voice, registering not only differences in time, place and outlook and the thought patterns of other cultures,[10] but also individual temperaments as its teachers wrestled with 'the misery and grandeur of human beings'[11] and the greater divine mystery within which they saw all human life being held.

Ecclesiastes beckons, but not before we have noted an interesting fact alluded to in the concluding pages of the previous chapter. In the wisdom literature of Israel, Wisdom is a She.[12] In Proverbs 8, Wisdom is personified as a woman who urges upon others the duty of right action (v. 6), the love of truth (v. 7) and the importance of sound instruction that is better than jewels (v. 11). At the crossroads (a telling reminder that every day we are confronted with choices that will shape us as persons in some way) and by the gates in front of the town (another reminder that the practice of wisdom belongs as much in the public square as in the private domain of the heart), she takes her stand and declares:

> The LORD created me at the beginning of his work ... Ages ago
> I was set up, at the first, before the beginning of the earth.
> When there were no depths I was brought forth ...
> Before the mountains had been shaped ... I was brought forth ...
> When he marked out the foundations of the earth
> then I was beside him ...
> I was daily his delight, rejoicing before him always.
>
> (Prov. 8.22–25, 29–30)

We are left in no doubt here concerning the origins of Wisdom: she exists before all things, a co-worker with the Lord of all times and seasons.

Ecclesiasticus echoes this claim: 'Before the ages, in the beginning, he created me, and for all the ages I shall not cease to be' (24.9). The implications and consequences of such a claim, viewed through the eyes of faith, are startling, even thrilling. The universe cannot be ordered without Wisdom (or, for St Paul, without Christ). She calibrates the stuff of the cosmos and her role 'makes craftsmanship and, later, modern science possible'.[13] That the world today is held to be intelligible, that its workings and mysteries are amenable (up to a point) to scientific scrutiny and investigation is, in part, due to the intellectual curiosity and convictions of an ancient wisdom tradition that saw the world as a competently created artefact reflecting the mind, artistry and intention of its maker.

Returning now to that very singular voice identified in Ecclesiastes, can we say that Qoheleth endorses this view of the universe? A cursory reading of the chapters suggests he does. With its 40 occurrences, the word 'God' is one of the most frequently used words in the book – though interestingly, 'Qohelet never uses the name of Yahweh, Israel's God'.[14] For Qoheleth it is God who has fixed the whole system: he is in control of all that happens under the sun. Human life owes its existence to him (Eccles. 5.17; 8.15; 9.9); wealth (6.2) and pleasure (2.24) are his gifts, along with intelligence and wisdom (2.26). If we read more carefully, however, it becomes evident that Qoheleth is not in fact talking about the cosmos as such but about all that happens in human life, in that dark and impenetrable world where so often individuals go astray. Here he finds much that is baffling and absurd – an affront to both reason and the providential ordering of things affirmed elsewhere in Judaism. With his emphasis on fate and fortune (mentioned nowhere else in the Bible, since they are pagan concepts) and his analytical approach to events and happenings and what might be good for mortals, Qoheleth's voice becomes touching and personal, amounting to 'fragments of a confession'.[15] In 12 brief chapters, Ecclesiastes continually circles around four basic insights that, taken together, constitute a sacred text and a philosophy that have no obvious comparison elsewhere in Scripture. Summarized, they amount to this:

1 a rational examination of life seems unable to locate any satisfactory meaning: everything is 'vanity';
2 God determines every event;
3 mortals are unable to discern or make sense of these decrees – the works of God in the world;
4 the necessity of realism in the face of loss.

A sobering compilation, and we can see why some biblical commentators occasionally express surprise that Ecclesiastes managed to find its place in the canon of Scripture given its mordant perspectives. A book that opens with the disarming assertions that all labour is vanity (1.3), all endeavours wearisome (1.8), and that people of any age are not long remembered after their death (1.11), does not seem a helpful or encouraging manual for the church study group or the happy hour of Sabbath morning. We have to dig a little deeper into the text to make some sense of these daunting estimations.

First, that word 'vanity' should not be mistaken for its more conventional description of an excessive belief in one's own abilities or attractiveness to others. Before the fourteenth century it simply meant futility and this is how the term is employed by Qoheleth. Many, even most, human activities and aspirations are futile, useless and fleeting, amounting to little more than 'pursuing the wind'. Toil does not necessarily bring a decent reward, justice is frequently denied, tears are not wiped away and honesty seems not to pay. Moreover, in an uncertain world where 'there is nothing new under the sun' (1.9), the future looms as an uninviting prospect over which we have no control. This clearly is not the voice of one who is thrilled by the promise of a glad, confident morning, but neither is it the bitter articulation of the nihilist. Qoheleth does not suggest that we torch house and home because nothing really matters very much. Rather (and here is the big surprise), he finds in the flux of things a certain constancy, something that mysteriously underpins every event. He ascribes to this phenomenon the neutral word 'time' – a time and an hour have been set, and for everything there is a time and a way (8.6). This conviction surfaces again and again: time and chance happen to all and behind the days of prosperity and adversity lies the hand of God, the divine activity that 'has made everything suitable for its time' (3.11).

The poignancy of our situation lies in our inability to penetrate the veil. Even if there is an invisible hand controlling affairs, and even if we believe this to be the case, our predicament arises from our inability to find out or discern what God has done or is doing. This is not our fault and it is not through lack of trying. However much we toil in seeking understanding, 'no one can find out what is happening under the sun' (8.17). We fail to register the time and 'like birds caught in a snare, so mortals are snared at a time of calamity' (9.12). Old age and death will also come soon enough: in a passage of great, if melancholy, beauty, that stands comparison with the universality of Shakespeare, Qoheleth points us to our human end:

25

Remember your creator in the days of your youth, before the days of trouble come, and the years draw near when you will say, 'I have no pleasure in them'; before the sun and the light and the moon and the stars are darkened and the clouds return with the rain; on the day when the guards of the house tremble, and the strong men are bent, and the women who grind cease working because they are few, and those who look through the windows see dimly; when the doors on the street are shut, and the sound of the grinding is low, and one rises up at the sound of a bird, and all the daughters of song are brought low; when one is afraid of heights, and terrors are in the road; the almond tree blossoms, the grasshopper drags itself along and desire fails; because all must go to their eternal home, and mourners will go about the streets; before the silver cord is snapped, and the golden bowl is broken, and the pitcher is broken at the fountain, and the wheel broken at the cistern, and the dust returns to the earth as it was, and the breath returns to God who gave it.

(Eccles. 12.1–7)

This is not a religion for softies, but there is an odd consolation to be found in its admonitions. We are urged to take nothing for granted, to enjoy the health and vigour of our vital years and to remember the Creator who gave and will receive our human life-breath. In the days that are allotted to us, there is also time for love and pleasure:

Go, eat your bread with enjoyment, and drink your wine with a merry heart; for God has long ago approved what you do. Let your garments always be white; do not let oil be lacking on your head. Enjoy life with the wife whom you love, all the days of your vain life that are given you under the sun, because that is your position in life and in your toil at which you toil under the sun. (Eccles. 9.7–9)

This is a good moment to pause in order to deal with the difficulties Ecclesiastes has raised so far. Too many contradictions are not good for the mind seeking a more serviceable wisdom than appears on offer here. So many questions arise: can Qoheleth be taken seriously in all his contrariness, ambivalence and gloom? In what way is he really a helpful teacher to guide us in our comings and goings? On the one hand, he insists that such efforts really don't amount to very much, yet on the other, we should do what we can anyway and enjoy them because (in keeping with the Creator's mind) it's good that we should before the bleaker years draw nigh. Why does he seem wedded at some points to the earlier wisdom of Israel – that God exists and by his will upholds all that is – but in other instances appears an isolated voice, quite unable to help us locate or recognize the workings of God in the complexities and changes of life? In this respect, at least, he appears sincere: 'I said, "I will be wise", but it was far from me. That which is, is far off and deep, very deep; who can find it out?' (Eccles. 7.23–24). Such a strange and perplexing figure peers out of the pages of Ecclesiastes: not a Job howling laments at an empty sky and an absentee God, and not a Jeremiah convulsed with a sense that he has been deceived by the Most High (Jer. 20.7–9). Instead we behold Qoheleth, coming to terms with poker-faced life, displaying a quiet acceptance of its banes and blessings and 'a resignation that can leave no reader unmoved'.[16]

For the remainder of this chapter I want to take issue with Qoheleth's temperament, his questions and ours, with the aim of showing that there is a dark wisdom in his book that has continuing relevance for our time, when a sense of the tragic persists and the image of someone staring at a cobweb in the corner of the ceiling and feeling no desire to do anything 'is a symbol of a certain aspect of modern consciousness'.[17] Let me begin by making the obvious but necessary point that Ecclesiastes at key moments resembles the work of a troubled soul whose faith in God appears to expect little by way of help or revelation. The poet Rainer Maria Rilke comes to mind: 'Who if I cried, would hear me among the angelic orders?'[18] How can we account for this? Perhaps Qoheleth shares in the phenomenon of the faithful churchgoer who eventually rejects all the spiritual consolation he would seem to have earned. In the final stages of resignation or depression, what remains of the furniture of faith is put to one side and forgotten.

Commenting on the death of his mother and brother, the writer and playwright Samuel Beckett noted that they drew no value from their religion when they died; at the moment of crisis, it had no more depth than an old school tie. I know of such instances from my own ministry – individuals who have turned up in church for years, sitting, standing and kneeling their way through familiar rites, yet at the end of their life impervious to the consolations offered in the name of Christ. This detachment has less to do with logic or reason, I suspect, than matters of upbringing, individual sensibility, personal attitude and disposition, which combine to make a judgement on life and religion in a time of need or anxiety. In this respect, Qoheleth is in some ways the classic lonely rebel, deeply preoccupied with the perennial human problems of life but necessarily confined within the fallible circle of experience that is uniquely his and from which he negotiates his understanding of the world. He speaks the truth but, crucially, it is his personal, subjective truth – for him, no doubt, primary and self-authenticating – but not the final word, for example, on the possibility or impossibility of sensing the presence of God in the turmoil of existence.

Others in similar circumstances testify to a different kind of religious experience. Here is the distinguished American novelist and critic John Updike describing a moment of terror in Florence, where he was staying at the end of 1999, attempting to write an article on the future of faith for the *New Yorker* magazine:

> I woke in the night, and felt in the strange hotel room, fearful and adrift, near my life's end, a wide-awake mote in an alien, sleeping city ... To relieve my loneliness, I prayed asking to be allowed to sleep, without much expecting the prayer to be answered. But then I became aware of noise ... Lightning. Hectic

gusts. The rain was furious ... I was filled with a glad sense of exterior activity. God was at work – at ease, even within this nocturnal Florentine commotion ... My wife woke up, admired the solemn tempest with me, and went back to bed. I lay down beside her and fell asleep ... All this felt like a transaction, a rescue, an answered prayer.[19]

For Updike, God is at work in the storm. Qoheleth sees and feels differently. Not just in relation to God's activity but across the spectrum of what it is to be human, a melancholic haze attends his vision. He tells the truth but not all of it. He sees with an unflinching eye but he doesn't see everything under the sun despite his role as the teacher, who in the opening chapter of Ecclesiastes appears almost God-like as he surveys the passing scene (1.12–14). What he fails to see or register is that human life amounts to more than toil, tears or sporadic pleasure. These are his legitimate concerns but he makes no reference to equally real and valid dimensions of existence that bring deep contentment, happiness and hope: the sheer delight of the world around us with its glory and grandeur; the kind of day, the perfect day, that is so replete with warmth and beauty that, as Ralph Waldo Emerson said, 'To have lived through all its sunny hours seemed longevity enough'.[20]

Poets are the proper chroniclers of such giddy moments of joy or intensity when gratitude and wonder, rather than resignation, represent our response to a world that sometimes seems to stand at the intersection of heaven and earth. In her recent memoir, the American rock and roll poet Patti Smith records a memory from her very early childhood: upon seeing a swan rise into the air she was filled with an urge and desire 'to speak of the swan, to say something of its whiteness, the explosive nature of its movement, and the slow beating of its wings'.[21] The urge and desire remain with her still, along with a deep sense of thankfulness that continues to shape her creative vision.

No criticism of Qoheleth is implied in those comments. Ecclesiastes has an important place in my affections but its author is human with his particular foibles, burdens and pre-occupations. And this realization should come to us as a form of wisdom. Many influential writers of recent times – Sartre, Camus, Hemingway, Beckett and Graham Greene, along with prominent and dogmatic atheists of our day (whether scientists, writers or philosophers) – depict a world bereft of ultimate meaning that is indifferent to our concerns and flourishing. What I am suggesting here is that in keeping with Qoheleth, their jaundiced or attenuated view of things has something to do with their perceptions rather than the world itself. A useful insight, I think, in relation to the weight and significance we assign to words, from whatever source, that assert that nothing is worth doing and life is only ever a long drawn-out defeat.

Qoheleth, like the rest of us, sees 'in a mirror, dimly' (1 Cor. 13.12). If he has fixed views, it is also the case, I suspect, that because he is human, his inner life, like ours, is also fluid and restless, always in transition. Our experience, as the acclaimed American psychologist and philosopher William James noted, 'lives in the transitions',[22] and faith itself therefore will some-times change and may even be reformulated as life carries us forward to new and unexpected places. The contradictions of Ecclesiastes begin to make more sense once we grasp that its outlook is the work both of a 'considered life' and of a writer whose experience is pulled in different directions as it responds to the inconsistencies and bafflements of a puzzling world.[23]

James has another insight that can help us negotiate the conundrum of Ecclesiastes. In his book *The Varieties of Religious Experience* he introduces the terms 'healthy minded' and 'sick soul' to explain how individuals possessed of different instincts and attitudes approached the domain of religion. In the 'healthy mind' we are able to observe a temperament disposed to the bright side of life and a disinclination to ponder the darker aspects of the world. By contrast, the 'sick soul' is painfully conscious of the world's ills and tends to be discontented, searching for a purpose without necessarily finding one. We can recognize this distinction from our own experience. Some people seem to emerge from the womb to the sound of champagne corks popping, and as they grow they see the beautiful and good in everything and everyone. But they also seem unaware of life's cruelties, hardships and emptiness – the long periods endured by many that bring neither hope nor satisfaction. Others appear to be outsiders, finding the world tragic and intractable and ill disposed to our most basic notions of fairness and justice. For them there is frequently an ache or hollowness at the heart of things that finds no easy resolution.

James draws two important conclusions from his investigations. He notes that as a matter of fact most people seek to cultivate healthy mindedness as part of a religious attitude:

> We divert our attention from disease and death as much as we can; and the slaughter houses and indecencies without end on which our life is founded are huddled out of sight and never mentioned so that the world we recognise officially in literature and society is a poetic fiction, far handsomer and cleaner and better than the world that really is.[24]

This denial comes with a price, however. Averting one's eyes from evil is splendid for as long as it works. But it tends to break down as soon as melancholy or introspection expose deeper and more disturbing truths concerning our human situation. Even if we are not disposed to melancholy ourselves, James insists that 'healthy mindedness is inadequate as a philosophical doctrine because the evil facts which it refuses positively to account for are a genuine portion of reality and they may after all be the best key to life's significance and possibly the only openers of our eyes to the deepest levels of truth'.[25]

In the end, James concedes that the 'healthy minded' are likely to be happier and lead more fulfilling lives than most, but against this he maintains that the 'sick souls' have a deeper insight into the human condition. They are prepared to bear more of reality and, beyond pride, ambition and the world's glittering prizes, they have a clearer vision of the nature of things. 'The purely naturalistic look at life, however enthusiastically it may begin, is sure to end in sadness.'[26]

It is only recently that I have come across James's work in this particular area of psychology. On further reflection here, it strikes me as a strong endorsement of Ecclesiastes as a book of realism and its author as a man of principles and depth. He may be a 'sick soul', but as he surveys the passing scene there is an integrity and undeniable power in his estimation of things as he struggles to make sense of his times in which for him 'something is missing' and its absence hurts. Yet he persists in raising questions, sometimes in dialogue with the wisdom tradition he stands in and on other occasions going beyond it. If he seems to march to a different drum with his enquiry and conclusions, it is not fanciful to suggest that this may be evidence of his frustration, even disillusionment, with other schools of thought in Israel, that for him construct the world in excessively simplistic, rational or benign terms that fail to do justice to the unfathomable depths of existence and the fragile nature of any serious understanding of the world.

Qoheleth is a writer ahead of his time in this respect – proto-existentialist reflecting modern artistic and philosophical sensibilities that contrive the meaning of life as anti-climax. I suspect that he would be entirely at home with Kierkegaard's insistent questions in the realm of meaning:

> One sticks one's fingers into the soil to tell by the smell what land one's in; I stick my finger into existence – it smells of nothing. Where am I? Who am I? How did I come to be here? What is this thing called the world? What does the word mean? Who is it that has lured me into this thing and now leaves me there . . . If I am compelled to take part in it, where is the director? I would like to see him.[27]

Patently, in terms of certain forms of knowledge – science being the obvious case – we now know more about the world than either Kierkegaard or Qoheleth. We know that the universe is expanding, that space and time had their beginning in the phenomenon that we have no language for except the rather lame term 'big bang', and that the cosmos will ultimately undergo a fate that remains an open question in contemporary physics. We know that its intelligibility depends upon the existence of dark matter and energy (vast in scope) that we cannot see, and that at a point in time a capacity emerged in carbon-based life forms for morally significant actions, along with a propensity to do harm.[28] We know that there is waste and suffering within the evolutionary process, yet paradoxically both seem necessary in the working out of evolution that has made possible the emergence of consciousness and the finely calibrated conditions that sustain human life on earth.

All this we purport to know, and yet there is still no agreement concerning the fundamental questions of what we are and what we are for as human beings, as each one of us, by degrees, experiences and responds (sometimes in awe and with hearts on fire) to 'this great mystery of being, this great unfolding of ineluctable, irreversible time'.[29]

In relation to *this* question – perhaps above all others – Qoheleth and Kierkegaard remain our conversation partners and guides. They remind us that any adequate account of ourselves as reflective agents who are capable of anything, including the best, must include the fact that, as Aristotle noted long ago, we are meaning-seeking creatures destined to question[30] our inner lives and environment and desperate to know why life is sometimes a *via dolorosa* – a road of suffering that all must travel. The wisdom of Qoheleth lies in his ability to chart this road with exquisite and heart-rending precision without shirking the facts. He tells us that we are sentient creatures held fast in the clutches of time, that things and persons we care about are swallowed up, along with youth and promise, and that the people we love die. With our tremendous talent for deception on such matters, Qoheleth asks that we confront them with a steady gaze. This is the undertaking demanded of any proper human life and it is also a requirement of the Christian gospel. Rowan Williams writes that 'the resurrection is not properly preached without an awareness of the human world as a place of loss and a place where men and women strive not to be trapped in that loss'.[31]

This longing for something more than transience and living as a futile and sorrowful project also finds expression in Ecclesiastes. We sense Qoheleth yearning for the moment when it might be possible to say, 'See, this is new' (1.10). But for him, no such opportunity can arise, for there is only endless recurrence: 'what has been is what will be, and what has been done is what will be done' (1.9). He does not know that centuries later another voice will emerge, bearing the promise of the Christ, who will come to make 'all things new' (Rev. 21.5) in a heaven where God 'will wipe every tear from their eyes' (Rev. 21.4).[32]

3

The wisdom of the Incarnation: the prologue of St John's Gospel

———◆•◆•◆———

I see him sitting at a desk, suddenly falling back in his chair after writing the 251 carefully compressed words that announce his Gospel. Is he perhaps already conscious of the magnitude of his achievement – that in a kind of overture he wishes the reader to know that his telling of the story concerning who Jesus is only makes sense when viewed 'from a transcendent and eternal vantage point'?[1] Is he aware that in his articulation of a mystery – the unfathomable 'otherness' of God disclosed in the life of One who became everything to those 'who believed in his name' (John 1.12) – he is demonstrating the capacity of language to evoke a reality beyond its grasp and to give it 'a habitation and a name'? And, finally, as he prepares to relate his account of a public ministry culminating in unbelief, controversy, death and resurrection, can he have any idea that on the basis of his introduction alone, he is bequeathing to future generations a poetic and philosophical tract of inexhaustible meaning and imaginative power that will question the limits of our judgement and understanding? Possibly, in this respect, you have heard of the tourist who on looking round the National Gallery in London told an attendant that he did not rate the pictures on display. The attendant replied, 'It is not the pictures, sir, which are on trial.'

The man reeling in his chair from the implications of what he has just written is the author of the Fourth Gospel. Who is he? Some have argued that he is the apostle John, the son of Zebedee and one of the first disciples of Jesus (Mark 1.19–20).

35

Scholars have inclined to the view that he is a follower of John –
someone of the same name at Ephesus who 'played an influential
part in the life of the Church in Asia'[2] within two generations
after the death of Christ. The epilogue of this Gospel points
to an anonymous devotee of Jesus called 'the one whom Jesus
loved' (John 20.2) as the source and inspiration of this unique
work. His identity intrigues me a little, particularly as he seems
to wish to veil it,[3] but I am more impressed by the fact that his
book suggests a highly distinctive mind and forms an essential
part of the fourfold Gospel of a crucified and risen Lord.

Beyond intrigue and respect, however – so far beyond both
of these not insignificant things – I owe a debt of gratitude
to this author for a prologue before which 'I bow my knees'
(Eph. 3.14) and which remains for me the heart of the Christian
mystery. In a mere 18 verses, he invites us to contemplate a
blinding light that is not overwhelmed by the darkness and
testifies to the truth that something of the greatest significance
has happened among us. With some diffidence – because here,
as in other parts of the Bible, we tread on holy ground: the
burning bush (Exod. 3.2) and the Transfiguration come to mind
(Matt. 17.2) – my intention is to open up these verses in order
to discover what they have to teach us and why they affect me
so profoundly. Here is the opening section in its pomp and
pristine beauty:

> In the beginning was the Word, and the Word was with God,
> and the Word was God. He was in the beginning with God. All
> things came into being through him, and without him not one
> thing came into being. What has come into being in him was
> life, and the life was the light of all people. The light shines in
> the darkness, and the darkness did not overcome it.
>
> (John 1.1–5)

Nothing is surplus to requirement in this passage. A deliberate
and delicate concision shapes what is being affirmed, yet the
sparseness in no way diminishes its power to haunt the imagin-

ation and move the mind along what Whitman called 'the grand roads of the universe'.[4] From the outset John confronts us with the cosmic and mystical and challenges us to think about our evolutionary beginnings: that unprecedented moment when our universe was a trillionth of a trillionth of a trillionth of a second old, which led to the emergence of time and space and, eventually, solar systems and galaxies from a hyper-compressed 'singularity' (science has no other word for this phenomenon) no bigger than a billiard ball. We tend to put aside such thoughts, not because they are unfamiliar to us as we make our small steps through life preoccupied with mundane necessities but rather from a sense that we feel out of our depth when the conversation turns from matters of survival and happiness to baffling notions of deep space, other worlds and the farthest recesses of time. John, by contrast, is bold in relation to nature's unfolding and where we are to look for traces of the divine. He seems to trust his experience and his perceptions – for him they are gateways to the sacred – and, not least, the sense he has of himself, his unique identity, role[5] and perspective, even as he contemplates the immensity of everything. And he writes in the rhythm and style of Hebrew poetry, in such a way that another foundational text comes naturally to mind.

The first three words of the prologue, 'In the beginning', owe their inspiration to the opening of Genesis, the first book of the Hebrew Scriptures. There we read: 'In the beginning when God created the heavens and the earth . . . and darkness covered the face of the deep . . . Then God said, "Let there be light"' (1.1–3). Both texts begin from eternity, before the universe came into existence, and both ground its being in God, the majestic author of all things, for 'without him not one thing came into being' (John 1.3). The prologue arrests our thoughts before they run on, seeking to confine them to this one tremendous truth in order to be struck and dazzled by it: that God is a sphere whose centre is everywhere and whose circumference is nowhere; that in shedding forth universes his energies are not expended; that although his essence is mysterious we respond to it with fear and trembling, with unsatisfied longings and an intuition that in this word 'God' is to be found the 'meaning of meaning'.[6]

This feeling in the gut or pounding in the brain that expresses itself in an ache for the consolations of beauty or the desire to create is, in essence, an attempt on the part of the thinker, artist, musician or poet to imitate or recreate the biblical 'Let there be . . .': the primal assent and intention on the part of the divine maker attested in the opening verses of Genesis that there should be something rather than nothing, an ordered world rather than unending silence or chaos. The lure of transcendence, understood as the dizzying invitation to mimic, in some sense, the creative fire behind the constellations of the stars, has been the inspiration for the book of Job, Augustine's *Confessions*, Beethoven's *Missa Solemnis*, Shakespeare's *King Lear*, Michelangelo's Sistine Chapel, the novels of Tolstoy and Dostoevsky, and the protean genius of J. S. Bach that graces the world with music of incomparable splendour. Without religious art our inner and outward lives would be severely diminished. If we lacked the sacred spaces of the Blue Mosque in Istanbul or the cathedral at Chartres, which in their silence speak so eloquently of the divine, our human sensibilities would shrivel through lack of that 'oceanic feeling' that takes us beyond logic and reason into the realm of the mystical.

This is the world inhabited by the prologue: later in his Gospel John will present us with the historical person of Jesus, the itinerant preacher by the Sea of Galilee and in the streets of Jerusalem, as he breathes the air of Palestine. The prologue, by contrast, generates a different atmosphere through the contrast of light with darkness, spirit with matter, reality with appearance, grace and truth with law, and space with time. God suffuses its sentences and here religion confines itself to transcendence, before we get down to matters of ethics and human conduct.

A question seems inescapable: 'when John writes the word "God" to what or to whom is he referring?'[7] Not, I suspect, what congregations and clerics sometimes have in mind today when we glibly chatter on about God as a valued and familiar member of our circle of friends or, conversely, fall into an embarrassed silence, the sort of 'corner of the mouth' speech that suggests that for reasons bad rather than good we have no idea what we are talking about in relation to the existence or non-existence of God. James Jones, former Bishop of Liverpool, writes:

> We talk of God very casually and write about him as if he were a prescription for our ills. Even in church there's less sense of the majesty, the power and the glory of God. The awe has gone out of our worship and the proper fear has all but disappeared from our heart.[8]

To meditate on the prologue is to grasp that we can and should do better than this. It's not just that we have the examples of great artistry referred to earlier, creative lives that have fashioned remarkable things through their contemplation of or participation in the ineffable. It must also have to do with the biblical truth that we are created in God's image. Whatever our station in life, we are of equal and infinite worth and capable of moral acts because we can reflect the goodness enshrined within the divine. So it is that we give away our life jackets on sinking ships, run into burning houses to secure the screaming child, share our last morsel with one who has less and give without any expectation of reward. We can produce a Gandhi, a Mandela crushing the serpent's head of apartheid in South Africa, or an Aung San Suu Kyi accepting long years in confinement for the sake of democracy in Burma.

But we can do even more than this. We have the capacity for reflection, the gift of consciousness, the ability to question, ruminate and ponder and the endless curiosity that reflects something marvellous, even fundamental, in our kind. We are human; therefore everything is of interest to us. And the miracle is that we have the brain, the most complex artefact known to exist in the universe, to facilitate our capacity for enquiry and knowledge. There are more neurons in the human brain than there are stars in the Milky Way, which is another way of saying that the concentrated energies of consciousness that constitute the person we pass on the street or in the super-market aisle are no less and, arguably, an even greater marvel than our galaxy. In our forgetfulness and mental slumber, we fail to acknowledge that we are more God-like than we imagine or conceive. Part of our meaning as persons is precisely this: to entertain immensities – the world in a grain of sand, the particular light that falls on the stucco of the house on a street corner as evening falls, and the compelling human narrative (so hard to eradicate even in a time of scepticism and doubt) that binds us to the stars and insinuates that we have come from somewhere and are heading somewhere.

Such intuitions are not confined to the religiously minded alone: writing shortly after the discovery of a new particle using the Large Hadron Collider, the science writer and particle physicist Jeff Forshaw commented:

> I am struck by the astonishing beauty of the central equations in physics, which seems to reveal something remarkable about our universe . . . It leaves everyone who has studied these things with an overwhelming sense that the natural world operates according to some beautiful rules and that we are very fortunate to be able to appreciate them. We believe there are universal rules that would also be uncovered by sufficiently intelligent aliens on a distant planet; we are discovering something at the heart of things.[9]

From a quite different perspective, and close on two centuries earlier, the American writer and poet Edgar Allan Poe experi-enced a similar awe. In 1848, a year before his death and hollowed out by poverty, alcoholism and the pain of grief, he contemplated the night sky and heard in his mind the primal roar of the creation. He wrote a poem entitled 'Eureka' that amounted to a cosmology. With remarkable prescience, it anticipated the findings of modern science in relation to the origins of the universe. He reached his conclusions by poetic intuition and the peculiar mental faculties that set him apart from more prosaic minds. If he knew nothing of dark matter or dark energy, he detected in the rhythms of the universe a pounding life force and the sense of an ending – that the great void in all its visceral energy would one day cease to be.

He read the poem just once, to an enthusiastic audience in Richmond. We are not told if a questioner from the floor saw fit to ask him why he had written it, what had inspired him or convinced him that he had unlocked a great mystery – remember, the poem was called 'Eureka'. But it's not too fanciful, given what we know of Poe's imaginative reach, to suggest that his answer might have paid tribute to the fabulous workings of the mind, forever questioning the mysteries of human nature and the purpose of the heavens. And, great story-teller that he was, with an early grounding in religious instruction as a child,[10] he might also have acknowledged his debt to the first verses of Genesis and the prologue of John – the hammer blows of Scripture that bequeathed to his imagination and human history the belief that the universe had a beginning, and a cosmos had emerged out of nothing.

It is this suggestive power of the prologue, so allusive in its implications, that continues to fascinate me. John speaks of a beginning and God. A space separates these mysteries in the opening lines of his text and in it he sets down a concept, the eternal Word or Logos, a Greek noun with a rich past that he does not explain. It is here that the intrigue begins. The semantic possibilities of this term are huge, and even Poe with his febrile imagination and love of detective fiction might have struggled with its theological and philosophical meanings. Since John declines to provide a definition, here is one from the fourth century:

The Logos produces a single melody . . . holding the universe like a lyre, draws together the things in the air with those on earth, and those in the heaven with those in the air, and combines the whole with the parts, linking them with his command and will, and thus producing in beauty and harmony a single world and a single order within it. He extends his power everywhere, illuminating all things visible and invisible, containing and enclosing them in himself (giving) life and everything everywhere, to each individually and to all together creating an exquisite single euphonious harmony.

The quotation is significant for three reasons. First, note the strong emphasis on beauty and order, which is also found in the prologue and held by both writers to be features of the Logos. Second, the words are attributed to Athanasius, Bishop of Alexandria, a powerful and influential figure in the early doctrinal controversies concerning the nature and person of Christ. In his famous work *De Incarnatione*, Athanasius expounds how God the Word, by his union with humankind, restored in us the image of God, and by his death and resurrection overcame death. It was Athanasius who, in his emphasis upon the prologue, gave rise to the liturgical celebration of Christmas as not simply the birth of Christ but the coming of the Logos to the world, 'and its taking human nature upon itself to redeem it'.[11]

Third, to ponder these facts is to be struck by the paradoxical outworking of the significance of Logos in the Christian mind and imagination. On the one hand it is the source of harmony, giving light to all things, and on the other, beginning with John, it is the idea – or, as Athanasius would have insisted, 'the saving truth' – lying behind the debates and deep antagonisms among Church leaders at the ecumenical councils of Nicaea (325), Chalcedon (451) and Constantinople (553). In his recent book tracing the evolution of Christianity in the first four centuries, Geza Vermes notes that such controversies 'all arose from the first message enunciated in the Fourth Gospel and especially in its Prologue's startling claims that Jesus was the Word and the Word/Logos was God'.[12]

This is the claim that we hear in church each Christmas as John's momentous words pierce the midnight liturgy with their ancient power. As I read them aloud they invariably prompt in me (and I hope in assembled listeners) the awe that is appropriate to their origins. Here is a writer registering a cosmic shift in human understanding concerning how things come to be and who Jesus is.

Because I have a need to get behind these words without in any way diminishing their beauty, the question of where John derives his inspiration is never far away. Earlier, we identified Genesis as one source – entirely feasible if we accept the possibility that John was a Hellenized Jew who, like St Paul, benefited from a Palestinian education. Ancient rabbinic interpretations of the opening words of Genesis – '*In* the beginning' – offer a twofold understanding of the phrase. It can mean either 'with Wisdom' or 'with the Word', the work of divine creation began. The former reflects Proverbs – 'the Lord by wisdom founded the earth; by understanding he established the heavens' (3.19) – while the latter points to the divine Word and the commands through which the different created realities come into being in the first chapter of Genesis. The rabbis also believed that the Law of God was in existence before the world began and, in a leap of imagination, supposed that God consulted the Torah as a template for bringing the world into being. The Psalms corroborate such belief, with their testimony to the word of Yahweh as the power by which he created the universe and sustains it in being (Ps. 33.6, 9; 147.15). The same divine word comes to the prophets as they submit to a compelling mandate that they must obey (Jer. 1.4–10; Amos 3.8). It is an active, creative and renewing force destined by God 'to accomplish that which I purpose, and succeed in the thing for which I sent it' (Isa. 55. 11).

Taken together, these various examples of Jewish scripture and interpretation provide an intelligible framework for John in relation to an understanding of the creative role of the Word. But we have to remember that he is still employing a Greek noun in the prologue – the Logos, which Greek philosophers such as the Stoics saw as the fiery, divine breath that organized the whole of reality. To understand John's choice of terminology a little more, we need to make an acquaintance with a contemporary of John the Baptist and Jesus; like them, he was a Jew, but he inhabited a quite different intellectual world.

The Jewish philosopher Philo of Alexandria (20 BC–c.45 AD) came from a wealthy family. As an expositor and interpreter of Jewish texts, he took upon himself the task of translating the essence of Semitic stories into another cultural idiom. Influenced by Plato, he produced commentaries on Genesis and came to believe that the Word or Logos of God was the rational impulse that structures the universe,[13] and that when we catch a glimpse of this in creation, we come to the recognition that God is 'higher than a way of thinking, more precious than anything that is merely thought'.[14] His philosophy is touched by mystical experience and, 'like a priest in one of the ecstatic mystery cults',[15] he is seized by rapture:

> I . . . have suddenly become full, the ideas descending like snow, so that under the impact of divine possession, I have been . . . filled with frenzy and become ignorant of everything, place, people, past, present, myself, what was said, and what was written. For I acquired expression, ideas, an enjoyment of life, sharp-sighted vision, exceedingly distant clarity of objects such as might occur through the eyes as a result of clearest display.[16]

In touching the holy fire, Philo's writing served as the inspiration that would enable early philosophers and theologians to create some of the defining beliefs of Christianity and adapt a Jewish faith to the Graeco-Roman world. Justin (100–160) argued in his two *Apologiae* that Jesus was the incarnation of the Logos which had always been active throughout history, inspiring Greeks and Hebrews alike. It had spoken through

Plato and Socrates as well as the Hebrew prophets, and as
Irenaeus, a later 'father' of the Church, would claim, the writings
of Moses were actually the words of Christ, the eternal Logos,
who had been speaking through him.[17]

Such claims and convictions brought a new and poetic dimension to the Christian message that would elevate the divinity
of Jesus and fuse Jewish and Greek conceptions of the Logos.
In his *Confessions*, Augustine compares the opening verses of
John's Gospel with the writings of Plato, and informs us that
he found identical notions in both the Gospel and the Platonists,
though not in identical words.[18] Without Philo, and the prologue that speaks of the Word, and the mission of that Word
in a world not easily disposed to heed its appearance and truth,
early Christianity would have been quite different. It is John,
indebted as we have seen to a range of ideas and experiences,
who gives to the Church in its formative period a new concept
in the form of the Logos. And to the person of Jesus he confers
a new status that takes him beyond the role of Jewish Messiah
or holy man to that of a 'Christ-like God'.[19]

What are the lessons – better still, the wisdom – to be derived
from this exploration of the sources that lie behind the prologue
and the truth declared by John that can be likened to an overflowing river 'joined by streams which had taken their rise elsewhere'?[20] In order to answer the question our tools of investigation
can be laid aside in order to return to the image that opened
this chapter – John at work on his scrolls, momentarily taken
aback by what he has written. Perhaps you can hold this picture
in your mind, as I'm doing now even as I write these words.

We are looking at a scene that touches upon a venerable
tradition of what it is to be a theologian. The man before us,
the author of the Fourth Gospel, was called 'the Theologian',
according to graffiti on the ancient church at Ephesus, and also
in the dedications of many English churches and cathedrals.
When next I visit the great cathedral of St John the Divine in
New York, I may well find myself wondering how many of the

congregation or visitors realize that the ascription 'the Divine' means 'the Theologian'. Implied in the title is a particular kind of learning, perhaps that of the disciple who leaned on the breast of his Lord at the Last Supper and came to know what he knew through such close and affectionate intimacy. John is a friend of God – a designation often associated with the saints – and he has come to this friendship through prayer, attentive waiting and reflection. He is a theologian who does not disparage the knowledge to be gleaned from books – note the scrolls on his table – but his understanding is shaped in part by his spirituality, and his theology is as much a matter of the heart as of the head. As he sits at the table, the prologue completed, he is in the silent presence of the Eternal Beyond, the God of grace and truth, and in what follows he will write what a former Archbishop of Canterbury once described as 'the most beautiful book in the world'.[21] He will make no further reference to the Logos – he has already referenced it four times in his introduction – but he will convey to his readers all that he has seen, heard and experienced concerning the Word of life that has made him free (John 8.32). And he will do all this in an attitude of prayer, conscious that above all he wishes to glorify God through his testimony, and that in this endeavour he will find what he most desires.

> I can only find satisfaction in him.
> My heart, to love him;
> my will, to do his will;
> my mind, to glorify him;
> my tongue, to speak to him and of him;
> my eyes to see him in all things;
> my hands to bring whatever they touch to him;
> My all only to be a real 'all': because it is joined to him.
> And this will be utter joy: no man can take it away . . .
>
> Thanks be to God for being what He is, for showing
> Himself to me.[22]

This prayer is not the work of John; in fact, as will become clear in a moment, it's not strictly speaking a prayer. But this is not a lesson in grammar and I'm content to suggest that the spirit of John courses through it with each reference to love, life in its fullness, glory and the inward joy that is not diminished by the world's taint. And only to 'suggest' is actually a little timid on my part, for I happen to know that the author of the above lines spent a lifetime meditating on and preaching the religion of the Incarnation that we have come to identify with John's Gospel.

In September 1929, shortly before he was ordained to the priesthood in Farnworth parish church, a rather shy and awkward young man attended an ordination retreat in Oxford. During a time in meditation he wrote a note in pencil that still survived some 60 years later.[23] It constituted his heart's desire and his estimation of the essence of priesthood. Its contents are already known to you, but in a postscript he goes on to record his gratitude to the many who had formed his heart and mind: eminent teachers, pastors, family and authors of the Bible.

A little more than a year later he was working hard as sub-warden of Lincoln Theological College. His lectures enthralled students and in chapel they encountered a priest 'who had a manifest and rare mystical sense of the immediate presence of God, a presence so brilliant that it could almost overpower'.[24] In his teaching, the glory of God mediated through the Fourth Gospel and the discourses of Plato became a central theme. Silence was his guide. The story goes that an applicant for a college place came before him for interview. For 15 minutes the prospective student and interviewer sat opposite each other without a word being exchanged. The sub-warden finally said, 'I think you will find Lincoln rather a quiet place',[25] and this remark ended the interview. The sub-warden, Michael Ramsey, would later become the hundredth Archbishop of Canterbury since Pope Gregory the Great sent St Augustine to these shores in AD 597.

At this point parallels become inescapable. Ramsey and St John are theologians who commune with the divine and make God

47

near. They speak of the deepest things without recourse to technical language. Their thought is the consequence of silence and prayer, of philosophical riches appropriated from other schools of thought and gratitude for what has been disclosed to them in Christ. There is a discernible awe in their evocations of what they have seen. When they say a thing is *tremendous* or *exciting*, such is the case, for it is the truth of Christ rather than the truth about Christ, often summed up in a compelling phrase or sentence, that is communicated in their writing: 'There was a man sent from God, whose name was John' (1.6); 'He was in the world . . . yet the world did not know him' (1.10); 'But to all who . . . believed in his name, he gave power to become children of God' (1.12). Ramsey makes such utterances his own and, without knowing it, is led by the hand of God to speak of a Christ in whom we are 'allowed to see not only the radiance of God's glory, but also the true image of man'[26] – what it might mean to grasp our true stature as creatures in God's image. In the light of this revelation, 'And the Word became flesh' (1.14), both theologians are aware of an experience – a state of being – that does not lead them directly into action but will, from that moment, lead them 'to think and act in a new way'.[27] In all they do and seek to do from this point, rooted in their minds is the realization that in Christ, grace and truth have kissed the earth in a way that changes things for ever:

> Come to Bethlehem once again:
> see the stable – see the child. Knowing
> that he is God made man, knowing
> that he who was rich has become
> poor for us, let us kneel in the
> darkness and cold that is the
> symbol of our blind and chilly
> human hearts and say *in a new way*:
> 'yours is the kingdom, the power
> and the glory forever.'[28]

The italics are mine. They serve to remind us that in seeing the Incarnation through the lens of wonder, we become aware that the prologue of John is an invitation to a deeper conversation, a form of discipleship that can say the Lord's Prayer in the knowledge that glory, not shame or dissolution, constitutes our hope and end, and that the way of simplicity and sacrifice is the fulfilment of love's work. To know, to really know and therefore live in the conviction that 'the grace of God has appeared, bringing salvation to all' (Titus 2.11) is, at once, to be dissatisfied with lesser gods and resolved only to wait and work for 'the glory of our great God and Saviour, Jesus Christ' (Titus 2.13).[29]

Wonder is the key here – a wonder that for later hymn writers 'struck the world amazed,/ It shook the starry frame'.[30] Without this capacity or openness to experience – what Newman describes as the religious duty of taking 'a poetical view of things'[31] – the luminous opportunities of life where the infinite is to be found in everything will go unrecognized. The wisdom of the prologue lies in its capacity to bring about a shift in our imagination that can give birth to a deeper love. Such a transformation will be reflected in our character and disposition towards others: we shall no longer be content in a world of hurts and divisions to cultivate our inner peace and purity at any cost – 'to pass through a battlefield with a rose in my hand'.[32] And it is just possible that in the way we worship there will be a new attentiveness, evident in our singing, our stillness during prayer, our alertness to Scripture and sermon, even our walk as we move towards the altar of God.

Imagination should not be confused here with its twin impostors fantasy and make-believe. It is rather the capacity to stand before any reality, sublime or severe, and to have a sense of what God is asking of us. Even the greatest can be slow to grasp this. The night before his conversion to Christianity, C. S. Lewis took a long walk with J. R. R. Tolkien, author of *The Lord of the Rings*. As a Christian, Tolkien sought to persuade Lewis of the credibility of faith in Christ, but the sceptic kept mounting objections. Tolkien countered them finally with a simple statement:

'Your inability to understand stems from a failure of imagination on your part!' Lewis yielded and his perceptions were cleansed.

In this chapter I have placed quite a big bet on the poetry
of the prologue and its ability to take us beyond tired pieties.
I have indicated how for later centuries it became talismanic
for some religious parties as they sought to give the fullest
expression in creeds and councils of the Church concerning
what they believed about Christ and his identification with
God. I cannot finish without quoting some moving and pro-
vocative lines from a poem by Goethe; set alongside the opening verses of the Fourth Gospel, they invite us to reflect more
deeply on the familiar:

> Jesus felt purely and thought
> Only of the One God in silence;
> Whoever makes him into God
> Does outrage to his holy will.[33]

There is an affirmation and a rebuke here: an endorsement
of the picture we have of One who was indeed pure in heart
and sought God in the silence of Galilee. But there is also
a questioning of those who came after and allegedly turned
a charismatic Jewish teacher into a deity in a way that Jesus
himself would neither have recognized nor endorsed. The truth
is, I believe, rather more complex, but Goethe's lines challenge
me (and I hope you) to think again about who Christ was and
what he means for us today.

The prologue of John sets before us a great mystery. The
contested deliberations of the early centuries sought to make
sense of that mystery, both in its earthly life as manifested
in Jesus and in its subsequent impact upon the immediate
generation of believers and those who came after. Great acts
take time, sometimes even centuries. So it proved for those who
looked back on Jesus and came to see in him the human face
of God. Their experience, informed by reason, imagination and
devotion, would not allow them to do otherwise.

4

The wisdom of St Paul

As a world religion Christianity remains strong and vibrant. Over the past century its followers have doubled in number to more than 2 billion and this figure is expected to increase at a dramatic pace for the foreseeable future. An unlikely outcome for a movement that seemed doomed as an uncomprehending crowd shouted, 'Crucify him!' on the first Good Friday. And, more significantly, utterly inconceivable without one man: an apostle riddled with contradictions and endowed with mercurial qualities, who to this day continues to evoke awe, gratitude, misunderstanding and dislike in pretty even measures.

This man's achievements and legacy remain the stuff of fierce debate in the Church and beyond. In the pews of ordinary parish churches, the letters he wrote to fledgling Christian communities are heard dutifully but rarely with joy. Earlier centuries saw him differently. In the National Archaeological Museum in Florence, a bronze lamp has been preserved from an aristocratic Italian villa of the late fourth century. The lamp takes the form of a boat. In the stern sits St Peter at the tiller, to whom, we recall in the Gospels, Jesus gives the keys of the kingdom (Matt. 16.19). But there is another figure, standing in the prow. He is guiding the boat before the wind, and his name is Paul. We are not to misunderstand the message: Peter steers but it is Paul who guides the vessel through the uncharted waters of a tempestuous world.

It is the wisdom of this man, Saul of Tarsus, who became Paul in a moment of mystical transformation, that I wish to share in this chapter. I do so as a teacher well aware of the accusations routinely levelled at him – bigot, misogynist, homophobe, and distorter of an earlier and simpler message of love and forgiveness preached by Jesus – but also as an admirer and fellow traveller whose life and ministry owe much to this enigmatic, vulnerable and inspiring apostle, tossed about on heaving seas, risking everything for the Christ who had possessed him on the road to Damascus.

Before I try to distil the wisdom I find in Paul, it's important to recall his accomplishments. They are so extraordinary that it's easy to overlook them. Without his conversion, and the many years of missionary journeys that exposed him to hardship, violence and unceasing agitations, Christianity would almost certainly have remained in Jerusalem as a new and fragile expression of Judaism, drawing on the memory of a Galilean preacher and exorcist, whose declared mission was 'only to the lost sheep of the house of Israel' (Matt. 15.24). It is Paul who takes up this crucified and risen life and its Jewish inheritance. He weaves their stories, truths and moral precepts into the hearts and imaginations of the wider world he sought to transform in the name of a Saviour to whom everyone – Jew and Gentile – could look for salvation. Paul, more than any other figure in the New Testament, is responsible for the inception and spread of Christianity as a new religion, grounded in the God of Israel, disclosed in Jesus. Half (yes, incredibly, half!) of the New Testament confronts us with Paul, through his letters and in the book of Acts, where he figures prominently in 16 of its 28 chapters.

It's Paul who shapes the history of Christianity, through the impact of his writings on the movers and shakers of the Church. In the fourth century, St Augustine, in a moment of graced illumination, encounters a passage in Romans (13.13–14) that brings him certainty and light after dissipation and darkness. He will become the seminal voice of the Church of the first millennium. In the sixteenth century, Martin Luther has a similar experience, while preparing lectures on Paul, which will lead to the Reformation and the eventual emergence of the Lutheran Church. John Calvin (no less a luminary than Luther in the annals of Protestantism) makes Paul the cornerstone of his theology, while two centuries later in England, John Wesley experiences a strange warming in his heart as he listens to a reading of Luther's commentary on Romans. His conversion proves momentous. His prodigious energies lead to the birth of the Methodist Church, initially as an adjunct household of faith to a Church of England that will prove hostile to its founder's reforming zeal and passion for evangelism and the poor.

My point? Paul matters hugely to any informed and balanced understanding of the Christian faith and the fascinating trajectory of its history. Whether we bring questions, accusations or bouquets to his feet, we make a colossal mistake if we ignore him or refuse to enter into a more serious negotiation with the workings of his mind and the fierce passion that animates his deepest convictions. There is, admittedly, a problem: Paul makes strenuous demands on the reader. We can be moved by his hymn to love (1 Cor. 13) and encouraged to persevere in the face of loss and adversity in the light of Romans 8 (vv. 31–39) and its colossal wager on the indestructibility of the Christian hope. Sometimes, however, his texts baffle or confuse us, and the fierce urgency of his voice jars. To be crucified with Christ or confronted with the righteousness of God proves to modern ears less appealing than the Gospel stories of shepherds and sheep, the birds of the air, the lilies of the field and the Samaritan who proved such a jolly good chap. Paul has fewer stories and less patience than the Jesus who seemingly has time for everyone, especially the wearied and troubled (Matt. 11.28). We disengage from the majority of Paul's letters and his strictures concerning the flesh and in so doing ignore the awesome and devastating implications of the whole. The loss is ours. Paul is difficult but no more so than the Jesus of the Gospels, who is not just a consoling teller of tales, and considerably more disturbing than conventional piety and preaching often allow.

Perhaps this is the beginning of wisdom in relation to Paul – that we think we know him or have understood him when, in fact, neither is true. So we have the task, opportunity and privilege of starting over, of conceding that the Paul we pass by on the other side is frequently a caricature of our own devising or prejudice; we need to come as willing learners if we are even to begin to grasp his vision of the crucified Jesus who becomes his inner light and life. The good news is that we are not the first to have marginalized Paul in our thinking or devotion to the great cause that is Christianity. In fact, a plausible case can be made that in view of the sweep and depth of his thought – 'too ecstatic, too jagged, too hither and thither to be described . . . as a system'[1] – any interpretation of his gospel (including this one!) is always a matter of work in progress. To enter Paul's world in any serious way is to be aware that we stand on holy ground and are close, closer than we had realized or conceded, to the mind and story of Christ.

When Oscar Wilde was a student at Oxford, he had to sit an examination testing his knowledge of Greek. He was set a difficult passage from the New Testament: Acts 27, which tells of the shipwreck of Paul as he journeyed to Rome, and his rescue, along with the crew, off the island of Malta. Wilde had to recite the translation of the extract aloud. He performed brilliantly, and one of his astonished examiners brought the proceedings to an early close with the words, 'That will be all, Mr Wilde.' He replied with his customary wit: 'Oh please, do let me go on, I am longing to know how the story finishes!'

Wilde makes an important point well. None of us knows how Paul's story ends. Luke does not relate, at the end of the Acts of the Apostles, what happened to Paul when he reached Rome. We learn nothing about his death, only that he lived there for two years preaching and teaching and proclaiming the kingdom of God (Acts 28.30–31). If you stand in St Peter's Square in Rome today and look at the basilica, you will see the carved statues of Peter and Paul testifying to their martyrdom

54

together in Rome under Nero in AD 64, along with many others who had become loathed and derided by the wider populace for their clinging to a new and detested religion. In his *Annals*, the Roman historian Tacitus records: 'Derision accompanied their end; they were covered with wild beasts' skins and torn to death by dogs; or they were fastened on crosses, and when daylight failed, were burned to serve as lamps by night.'[2]

Here the secular historian corroborates Paul's theology concerning what it means to be a Christian – a preparedness to be a spectacle to the world, fools for the sake of Christ and ready when the time comes to suffer and die. Writing to a divided community at Corinth that seems to be straying from the narrow and searching path of discipleship, Paul admonishes and encourages its members to emulate his example:

> For I think that God has exhibited us apostles as last of all, as though sentenced to death . . . To the present hour we are hungry and thirsty, we are poorly clothed and beaten and homeless and we grow weary from the work of our own hands. When reviled, we bless; when persecuted, we endure; when slandered, we speak kindly. We have become like the rubbish of the world, the dregs of all things, to this very day. (1 Cor. 4.9, 11–13)

The wisdom on display here is that of a radical religious contrarian – a man who has changed his view of the world completely, and is no longer persuaded or seduced by its standards that now seem inconsequential in the light of Christ's death and resurrection that alone give meaning to his life. It is the language of conversion, new beginnings and a form of existence predicated on the One who in the Gospel of John is 'the way, and the truth, and the life' (14.6). The romance and mystery of this transformation remain intact and alluring, despite the best efforts of organized religion over the centuries to flatten the language and quench the fire at its heart. That Paul retains the power to speak to our own fractured and tired religious sensibilities, that he is able to thrill us with images that soar and metaphors that quicken our moral imagination and make possible a Bach, a Benedict or a Michelangelo, mark him as a revolutionary of the first rank. He breathes a different air and urges us to set our minds on things that are above (Col. 3.1), to seek the mind of Christ in all things (Phil. 2.2).

To these ends he applies his best energies. The living out of the gospel dominates the second half of his life and lies behind the journeys, letters, joys and controversies that fill the New Testament. His canvas is vast and always there seem to be obstacles to deflect his purpose, or manifestations of his obdurate personality that might lead more liberal minds to eliminate him as the natural choice for a relaxed dinner party! The fact remains that through all this we see in his example and character nothing less than the loving wisdom of Christ. And in a world that has still to recognize fully the startling and beautiful implications of such wisdom, or thinks it odd or misplaced, this is a rare achievement that can seem excessive or unnecessary even to the initiated.

Some years ago the BBC televised a wonderful series based on the Barchester novels of Anthony Trollope.[3] His books bring a keen eye and wit to clerical life and ambitions in the nineteenth-century Anglican Church. Trollope is truthful but rarely cruel, and in the televised adaptation we are introduced to a bumbling bishop, his scheming wife, a simpering chaplain and an upwardly mobile archdeacon. There is also a godly warden, Mr Harding, an eccentric but endearing cleric in charge of an almshouse. He has a musical bent, a pastoral heart and a disconcerting propensity for speaking the truth. On one such occasion, an exasperated archdeacon is moved to comment, 'We really must excuse Mr Harding, he is prone to sporadic bouts of Christianity!'

Paul is certainly prone to this transforming contagion, yet he never rejects Judaism. We are told of his conversion four times – from his own lips in Galatians and three times in Acts. Significantly, his own account has no reference to a 'Damascus road experience' or a voice from heaven and his loss of vision. Instead, there is an emphasis on the unique and personal nature of the revelation to himself and that his experience of the risen Jesus owes nothing to the testimony of others, not even eminent apostles:

> For I want you to know, brothers and sisters, that the gospel that was proclaimed by me is not of human origins for I did not receive it from a human source, nor was I taught it, but I received it through a revelation of Jesus Christ . . . But when God, who had set me apart before I was born and called me through his grace, was pleased to reveal his Son to me, so that I might proclaim him among the Gentiles, I did not confer with any human being, nor did I go up to Jerusalem to those who were already apostles before me, but I went away at once into Arabia, and afterwards I returned to Damascus.   (Gal. 1.11–12, 15–17)

It takes Paul three years to come to terms with this revelation (great acts, we recall, take time): it is three years before he visits Jerusalem and confers with Peter and Jesus' brother James, leaders of a community based on 'the apostles' teaching and fellowship, the breaking of bread and the prayers' (Acts 2.42). It appears to be a patient community, staying in Jerusalem and waiting for the coming of the Lord. Paul opts for the road less travelled – a frenetic journey from place to place beyond the Jewish world, taking in merchants, slaves, soldiers, philosophers, wizards, synagogue leaders and sea captains. His travels still take the breath away when they are seriously pondered, yet somehow he finds time to write pastoral missives that will later contribute massively to the definitive teachings of the institutional Church.

The irony and the wisdom that surface here lie precisely in the fact that Paul is not inventing a new religion. He reminds, reproves and rejoices with the little platoons of believers that consume his time and patience yet also experience the gentleness of his affections and his intense wish that they should put away foolish things for something better – but at no point is he offering them a blueprint or a system or an extended formulation of faith. He is not a philosopher or church theologian trading in propositions or axioms that seek to define or defend the citadel of truth. In his letters, we see instead a pastor at work, an organizer with finely honed instincts, and a mystic and poet who has touched the rock and must speak of his experience of the crucified Jesus and his resurrection from the tomb. He must testify to what has happened to him, using words that should still arrest us today, for in Paul's estimation they constitute what it means and takes to follow the more radiant way: 'I have been crucified with Christ; and it is no longer I who live, but it is Christ who lives in me. And the life I now live in the flesh I live by faith in the Son of God, who loved me and gave himself for me' (Gal. 2.19–20).

I find myself returning to this passage again and again. I refer to it in lectures and sermons. It has become for me a defining text, along with the prologue of John. For Paul, the world's treasures amount to nothing when set against 'the unsearchable riches of Christ' (Eph. 3.8, AV). This is a staple theme in much preaching, of course, and also in the Gospels. Storing up worldly wealth does not make us rich in terms of the topsy-turvy values identified with the kingdom of God. But not too many sermons, in my experience, convey the heart-stopping reality, the sheer depth, profundity and implications of Paul's apocalypse for authentic Christian discipleship. Consider this: Paul has experienced a form of internal crucifixion, an inner death, an annihilation of his former self. A new Paul has emerged as proof of an internal transformation and a path has become possible to him that will make for a more abundant life. The old Paul has died and new life now means life in Christ. This pregnant phrase 'in Christ' is used by Paul more than 100 times in his letters; he uses the synonymous phrase 'in the Spirit' over 15 times. He sees baptism in the same light:

> Do you not know that all of us who have been baptized into Christ Jesus were baptized into his death? Therefore we have been buried with him by baptism into his death, so that, just as Christ was raised from the dead by the glory of the Father, so we too might walk in newness of life.   (Rom. 6.3–4)

Let's suppose for a moment that we changed our minds on that dinner party invitation we declined to send earlier to Paul on the grounds that he might be, well, just a bit too difficult, argumentative or demanding. Here he is at the table – tired after another long journey but actually more agreeable than we had imagined. The wine has soothed his more dyspeptic tendencies; he is asking about others (an endearing strain in his letters); in the candlelight he has the face of an angel (a fact attested by early Christian tradition), and to look into his eyes is to be confronted by the gaze of One who at supper also shared bread and wine with friends. He smiles (remember, believers were sometimes heartbroken when he left them) and then, by way of benediction as he prepares to leave, he relates again that moment on a road that changed him for ever and prays that our own experience may be grounded in that same reality of God. We show him to the door, sit down again at the table, pour another drink to compose ourselves and ponder the fact that we have been blessed and disturbed in a way we had not expected.

Paul has disconcerted us. He has asked us to revisit our experience in order to enquire if our inner life has something of the radiance and peace that comes from being 'in Christ'. No other option is available to him. No mention of creeds or formularies, no reference to specific denominational allegiances, no disputing precisely how bread and wine become the body and blood of Christ. Instead, there is just the hope and prayer that Christ is the centre of who we are and hope to become, and that we know this in our experience.

A rare moment follows: the scales do not quite fall from our eyes but we realize for the first time that we have encountered not only a formidable preacher and teacher who set the world on a different course, but a Jewish mystic insisting on the priority of prayer, experience and the inner life at the heart of our religious journey. Such things bind us to Christ and all those who have sought the vision of God. His one wish is that we should 'know the love of Christ that surpasses knowledge' (Eph. 3.19), so that we may be filled with the overflowing life of God. And he is reminding us, or possibly pointing out for the first time, that to be Christian is, in part, to seek union with God, to long for his presence and to experience within ourselves the renewing power of his Spirit.

I value Paul for many reasons, yet it is this fact – this foundational fact concerning the mystical dimension of his life – that I want to say more about. There is still a degree of confusion and suspicion around the term 'mysticism' and too often it is associated with the fuzzy, vague and ethereal: the Woodstock generation, flowing kaftans, flowers in the hair, preaching love and peace. Harmless enough, other-worldly, but not to be taken too seriously in a world driven by facts and the quest for conclusions. This is a poor and misleading caricature and we need to refer to a work mentioned earlier in Chapter 2 for a more precise and helpful term. William James, in *The Varieties of Religious Experience*, provides a working definition of mystical experience. He describes it in terms of union with the divine and the illumination that brings a deepened form of perception whereby the world is seen in a sacred light – in religious terms, full of God's glory (Isa. 6.3). Such experiences often include a sense of enlightenment, of moving from darkness to light or being awakened from sleep to an awareness of beauty or truth, rarely or never experienced before. They mark a departure from past ways of seeing and involve a form of knowing that is not to be confused with or reduced to intense feeling.[4]

James could be talking about Paul. We know about his Damascus road encounter, but elsewhere in his letters he speaks of his other experiences of the risen Lord (1 Cor. 9.1; 15.3–8) and being 'caught up to the third heaven'.[5] Paradise opens its gates and he hears things that 'are not to be told, that no mortal is permitted to repeat' (2 Cor. 12.4). There are no adequate words for this experience but it places Paul in the privileged company of those who have 'experiences of the golden world'[6] that are ineffable but, for the mystic, indubitably real. Just as he knows in a way beyond doubt or contradiction that his post-conversion call is from God, so too is he able to speak with perfect assurance of a transformation 'from one degree of glory to another, that comes from the Lord, the Spirit' (2 Cor. 3.18). Perhaps such passages have gone unnoticed in our reading of the New Testament, but they have led an eminent biblical scholar to insist that, 'Whoever takes away the mystical element from Paul, the man from antiquity, sins against the Pauline word: "Quench not the Spirit"' (1 Thess. 5.19, AV).[7] For myself, I have no wish to take this away: not because I fear the consequences of grieving the Spirit of God, but rather from the conviction that it is only through seeing Paul as a visionary and leader touched by another light that we can hope to grasp his significance and his worth.

How can we put this simply so that Paul remains available and helpful to us in the living out of the Way that characterized the earliest form of discipleship? Not all of us are mystics by nature or calling, but a common feature of our shared vocation is the sense we have that 'the Christian life is not just an outward allegiance; it is an affair of the heart'.[8] It is the heart that concerns Paul here: for all the searching depth and occasional convolutedness of his theology, there is this insistent strand in his letters. It points to the fundamental importance of our experience, the presence or absence of a yearning and desire for the living God, the deep gratitude and thanksgiving that come from knowing that all we have and own is sheer gift – 'Rejoice in the Lord always; again I will say, Rejoice' (Phil. 4.4) – and the joy that comes from a life and faith animated by the Spirit. And here's a surprise: never once does Paul use the word 'Christian' as he relates his vision of what it means to embrace the gospel. He talks instead of a new thing: the realm of being 'in Christ', of becoming 'a new creation' (2 Cor. 5.17) that testifies to the truth of the supernatural; 'you are in the Spirit, since the Spirit of God dwells in you' (Rom. 8.9). The

Spirit is sent into our hearts (Gal. 4.6) – the very centre of our being and the core of our deepest desires – and transforms what we want and are ready to give for the sake of Christ and the world.

Paul is not a sentimentalist, or an advocate of elevated or raw emotions as the defining features of this new life. His thoughts are never far from the message of the cross and the unending responsibilities of his role as pastor. God is not to be grasped as an emotional fix or uplift for the desultory spaces in our lives, and the Spirit is not a blanket term 'to cover a whole range of rich but too-fleeting experiences which may or may not be real'.[9] What he confronts us with instead is the question of what it is to be human and religious when too often the Church is seen and experienced as an assembly of depleted energies, long faces and shrill or angry voices. If we are to model God's new creation in a way that speaks of energy, hope and unceasing love, we must hold on to our brains and wrestle with the complexities and cares of our time, as indeed Paul does in his. But in addition to this, we must pay attention to our experience so that joy, feelings, and our long voyage of discovery are not dissolved in the name of religion into enervating duty, routine performance or a dopey adherence to creeds and empty convictions. Repetition can be the enemy of passion. Its antidote lies in the cultivation of experience – that 'inner essence, small, shining and precious' – nurtured by moments of vision when the sky above us becomes a mirror for an elusive something beyond that goes by many names, yet is ultimately experienced as the life and light of the world.

I wrote these words on 28 August 2012, the Feast Day of St Augustine, bishop and most esteemed theologian but also a student of Paul. For all his extensive writings and polemics, Augustine remains, at heart, a lover of Christ: 'Your word struck into my heart and from that moment I loved you'.[10] To be 'in Christ' is to be struck, pierced or wounded in some way. Not cajoled, informed or instructed, but opened up, transformed and recreated by the Spirit for joy and service to the rejected, the misused and the forgotten.

Paul embodies this truth. As a changed man, and never once using the word 'repent', his life now centres on the renewal of minds and human needs. He remembers the poor, organizes funds for the saints in Jerusalem, reminds us that the love of Christ leaves us no choice concerning those less fortunate than ourselves, and urges hospitality towards the stranger, the hungry and the thirsty. Right conduct is a natural outworking of a mind conformed to Christ, and in his letter to the Romans he devotes the concluding chapters to holy living. In the concern he shows for the humble and lowly (Rom. 12.14–21), we can hear Jesus speaking. Paul is handing on to us a tradition of things done by his Lord: bread and wine offered as a remembrance; a crucifixion and a mysterious rising; his appearances to the disciples and his victory over the final enemy of death.

We are to reflect on such things for they are of the first importance (1 Cor. 15.3). Our nature demands that we think them out in all their pros and cons and bring to them our best intelligence, for God has given us minds to love him. More than this, however, we have to return, time and again, to the actual deeds, the words said, the suffering embraced, the hope renewed in the dramatic and decisive memory of cross and empty tomb. The tokens of Christ's passion, death and resurrection – things done, shared and experienced – are commended to us by Paul as the spiritual template for our thinking and acting. This, in truth, can be an experience that is traumatic as well as liberating: 'an experience almost at times too hard to be bearable. The gospel did after all shatter its first bearer upon a hill of execution and what else can one expect, if in response to his call, one agrees to be sent forth again as a sheep among wolves?'[11] In the light of this truth, it is not surprising to learn that some declined to follow Jesus from the outset as his designated path appeared too strenuous for them (John 6.66). Paul is not to be mentioned in their number and therein lies his wisdom and his greatness.

No summing up of Paul is possible in a modest chapter, but let me offer you these final thoughts by way of reminder and encouragement. For all his contradictions and occasional lapses, it is a massive oversimplification to view him as in some sense a corrupter of Christianity, who has bequeathed an oppressive teaching, used by the Church throughout history to justify patterns of oppression in relation to women, gays and slaves. It makes no sense on the basis of what I've written here to view Jesus as good and Paul as bad. Certainly, he gets things wrong, makes mistakes and can be uncharitable to those with whom he disagrees – had I been around at the time, I would not have liked to get on the wrong side of him! But he is playing for the highest stakes; he is thinking as a pastor on the move, confronted by a sea of troubles and knowing that time is short (Romans 13.11–14). Against his critics, he can be remarkably inclusive in his thinking and relationships,[12] and should be acknowledged as one who taught and practised compassion for the sick and poor and insisted that having little by way of material wealth led to spiritual richness.

As a troubadour of Christ, Paul is, in the words of priest and poet George Herbert,[13] like every other all too human preacher of the gospel, 'a brittle, crazie glasse' who by the grace of God becomes a window through which we become intimately acquainted with who Jesus is. Perhaps he needed controversy and turmoil to evoke his genius. 'Examine the lives of the best and most fruitful men and peoples,' Nietzsche wrote, 'and ask yourselves whether a tree, if it is to grow proudly into the sky, can do without bad weather and storms'.[14]

We are back where we started at the beginning of this chapter. Paul is on the prow of the ship looking forward; the wind blows and the waves grow higher. But he will not be deflected from his call. He is and will always remain a faithful apostle of the Jesus who became his Lord. It is the Lord's face and not his own that Paul will reveal to all who will listen: a face that will change us for ever once we grasp what it really means to be 'in Christ'.

5

Wisdom and the ethics of reading

It's the morning after the fabled dinner party of the previous chapter – that deeply significant evening when an apostle *extraordinaire* descended unexpectedly upon our gathering to relate his hopes and experience and teach us that the mystery of salvation is bound up with our glad surrender to God. We are still talking about the encounter, feeling slightly embarrassed that we had not seen this side of Paul before, when a message comes through. It's from Paul, reiterating his thanks for our hospitality and what had been shared between us. He asks a small favour. In his hurry to be away and excitement at the conversation, he left a book in the sitting room. He doesn't tell us the title, only that he needs it. We oblige, of course, and one of us remembers a similar occasion in a New Testament letter when Paul requested a dear friend to bring him the 'cloak, books and parchments' he had 'left with Carpus at Troas'.[1] Again, no details are provided and an element of intrigue arises: why did he need scriptural scrolls at all? After all, 'he kept his Bible in the best place: in his heart and mind. He knew the Scriptures from childhood and could, and did, quote them freely.'[2] Paul often used Scripture in his letters without providing specific quotations. His references to Abraham and Genesis, to the Psalms and Isaiah, retell the story of Israel in the new dawn of Jesus and the Spirit. He is a serious reader immersed in a transforming narrative that has found its fulfilment in the Messiah he now wishes to proclaim to the whole world.

Serious reading is, essentially, what this chapter is about – the business of paying proper attention as we turn the page, follow the lines of text and make ourselves ready for the warmth, recognition and enlightenment that a particular assembly of words can sometimes evoke. This amounts to more than the simple pleasure of reading, of holding a book in our hands or appreciating its smell, texture, font or appearance. I'm a victim of all such temptations and hope to remain so for as long as my eyes and hands permit! What I'm concerned to convey here is the idea, even the belief, that in exercising a particular kind of responsibility or commitment to a book – we'll call this an 'ethic of reading'[3] – we can become better and wiser individuals.

Serious reading is a useful and necessary activity. It can open our eyes to beauty where once we saw only shadows, and illuminate our lives in such a way that we might even consider ourselves anew. In stories and characters both tragic and moving we can find patterns of behaviour and images of folly and faith (or the want of it) that mirror our own. We also come to see and understand ourselves better. More ready than before to ask questions concerning ourselves, we are also consoled by the knowledge that although the world is frequently cruel and mysterious, it is an incredibly meaningful place. An ethic of reading offers us more than a place of refuge or escape route as we switch on the bedside lamp after another crazy, depressing or frustrating day. It is the compass that can guide our self-discovery and our sincere but faltering attempts to extend ourselves and our moral sympathies to others.

I'm making a big claim here – one that might be easily misunderstood – so let me say as clearly as possible what I think serious reading amounts to. It is, of course, about books: not a long list of recommended texts or the books of the year that experts or critics tell us we must read if we wish to perfect the art of reading or impress others with our understanding of literature. This approach, with its emphasis on 'superior fare', can make aspiring readers feel self-congratulatory – 'we are the few who read the proper works' – or, more likely in my experience, it can deter them: 'how can we ever be worthy or even capable of such a high calling?' Lists of books, however great or good, are less important than the activity of reading itself. Whether we are tackling *The Odyssey* or *The Da Vinci Code*, the Old Testament or *Alice in Wonderland*, each constitutes literature and offers us a deeper way of connecting with the world, provided we bring a measure of reason, imagination and patience to the text.

But if we are going to a particular book in order to live differently, more creatively or authentically, then we need to treat the text well, be ready to negotiate difficult passages with care and look upon the whole work as a favoured guest deserving our hospitality. It's a matter of taking time to discern or discover what a particular story, poem or essay has to say to us and being prepared to revisit passages, or even whole books, more than once because they represent sources of wisdom or counsel. A generation ago, my college principal pointed out in a memorable sermon to the student body that not enough good books were read twice. Last week I heard him again after many years. At one point in his lecture, he mentioned an important work that he was beginning to understand only after reading it for the fifth time! His audience was, I suspect, daunted and impressed in equal measure by this revelation, but his underlying message was clear. To be a *reader*, as distinct from those who read, is to acknowledge the need on our part for space, quietness and, occasionally, solitude if we are to be enriched by reading and open to its promptings. Good books of any kind contain implicit questions that can reverberate in our minds for a lifetime, but they depend initially on our receptiveness. All writing can change us if we aspire to be generous and hospitable readers.

And 'there's the rub', as that most gifted of English wordsmiths once noted.[4] The sober facts are that we are locked into a culture that frequently allows little time for this kind of discernment and discretion and often leaves us unable to concentrate on anything for very long because of other distractions such as the ubiquitous lure of the internet and social media. Even devoted readers are not immune and within a few minutes of opening a book can begin to wonder if something has gone wrong with their brain. Nicholas Carr notes the problem:

> I'm not thinking the way I used to think. I can feel it most strongly when I'm reading. Immersing myself in a book or lengthy article used to be easy. My mind would get caught up in the narrative, or the turns of the argument, and I'd spend hours strolling through long stretches of prose . . . Now my concentration often starts to drift after two or three pages. I get fidgety, lose the thread, begin looking for something else to do . . . The deep reading that used to come naturally has become a struggle.[5]

And so, perhaps, say many of us. In a wistful moment we might even hark back to a golden age before the internet or even the printing press, when books were scarce and sustained attention was possible. The boy from North Africa who later became known to history as St Augustine spent many hours memorizing a handful of books, most of them by Virgil and Cicero. Books were treasured because they were in such short supply. Augustine analysed texts word by word, while St Paul, as we noted earlier, placed a high premium on the parchments he had left behind. Now the Amazon website produces a bestseller list running to 3 million and we wonder where to begin, or if it's even worth bothering! A little bit of delving, however, reveals that the problem of 'information overload' is not as new as we imagine.

In the thirteenth century, well before the German blacksmith and goldsmith Johannes Gutenberg introduced the printing press to Europe, a certain Vincent of Beauvais was busy producing a compendium of passages from his favourite authors, because 'the multitude of books, the shortness of time and the slipperiness of memory do not allow all things which are written to be equally retained in the mind'.[6] The sixteenth-century English philosopher Francis Bacon went a step further. In his essay

'Of Studies' he has this advice concerning the reading of books: 'Some books are to be tasted, others to be swallowed and some few to be chewed and digested . . . with diligence and attention.' History brings us reassurance at this point. It's all right and sometimes even necessary to skim (to *skim well* if we can) provided we reserve a place for deep attention. Not everything has to be read with patience and care but, following Bacon, we still need solitude or silence – the quiet room, corner or space – for the genuinely important words before us that should be taken seriously. Bacon seems to be asking a pertinent question: do we retain the capacity or desire to be an ethical reader?

Thinking about this reminds me of a famous passage in Charles Dickens's *David Copperfield*. As David reflects on a miserable childhood that made him sullen and dull, he recalls that one thing saved him – a small collection of books in a little room upstairs that kept his hope and imagination alive and helped ⌣ him to see beyond his suffocating circumstances: 'When I think of it, the picture always rises in my mind, of a summer evening, the boys at play in the churchyard, and I sitting on my bed, reading as if for life.'[7] There is an important clue in this last sentence: reading *as if for life* is the mark of the serious or ethical reader – one who knows that 'a book is like a mirror: if an ass looks in, you can't expect an apostle to look out'[8] – and if we really wish to further our humanity, reading can help.

To read is in some deliberate way to live a more engaged and passionate life that is consistent with that of the perennial student. The term 'student' is derived from study (in Latin, *studio*) and a quick search in a decent dictionary reveals that before its meanings changed,[9] the word 'studio' stood for affection, friendliness, devotion to another's welfare or pleasure and interest felt in something. It's not enough, therefore, just to pay attention to the text: the stakes are much higher. We are involved in an affair of the heart and therefore desirous that what we read should flourish within ourselves because we have adopted a loving stance towards it.

This is the language of aspiration, of course – the ethical reader we should like to be if only the internet, emails, the mobile phone and other seductive gadgets were not dissipating our desire! There are practical suggestions that can address such distractions – one or two will follow a little later – but what's harder is following them or even wanting to follow them, despite the intuition we have that it is precisely 'through difficulties we reach the stars'.[10]

One story that most of us know only through adaptations for stage and screen is *The Adventures of Pinocchio* – a nine-teenth-century Italian fable that has been reworked many times, most famously by Walt Disney in 1940. We think we know the story of Pinocchio, the mischievous animated puppet whose nose grows longer each time he tells lies – so long, eventually, that he cannot turn around in a room. A blue-haired fairy comes to his rescue by calling in a flock of woodpeckers and they chisel down his nose. So we say to our children that they should not tell lies if they wish to escape Pinocchio's fate, and for good measure add that a flock of anatomically engineered birds might not be on hand to carry out the cosmetic surgery! A simple morality tale, then? Actually, for all its success (and two Academy awards), the Disney film leaves out many of the most memorable chapters and avoids the darker elements of the story. Famous characters are changed: grumpy Geppetto, the poor man known for disliking children who carves Pinocchio out of a block of pinewood, is turned into a kind old man with a goldfish called Cleo and a cat called Figaro. An asthmatic shark that swallows Geppetto becomes Monstro the Whale, and the talking cricket that has lived in Geppetto's house for more than a century becomes the Jiminy Cricket we all remember. In keeping with the family values of the Disney corporation, Jiminy keeps pursuing Pinocchio with good advice. He wants the puppet to do the right thing on the shining path to maturity.

In the original story, Pinocchio is not so patient or obliging: when the cricket informs him that boys who do not obey their parents grow up to be donkeys, he throws a hammer at the insect and kills it! Oddly enough (particularly in view of my vegetarianism and vocation), I find this account more convincing, just as I find it disappointing that the film omits the most scary scene in the book: Pinocchio is refusing to take some medicine, but rapidly changes his mind when four rabbits 'as black as ink' enter the room intending to carry him off in a small black coffin as he will be dead soon. A macabre but compelling incident worthy of the best children's stories but insufficiently edifying for the Disney scriptwriters!

Pinocchio obliges because he wants to live. He is a puppet in a hurry. He began his life as a rebellious piece of wood but his wish now is to become a boy. He is precocious and impatient but not without decency. He promises Geppetto that he will go to school, after the old man makes him a new pair of feet. The old ones, we recall, are burnt off when Pinocchio places them on a stove, trying to keep warm after an irate neighbour has poured a basin of water over him, and falls asleep. On his way to school, however, he is distracted by the crowd congregating to see the Great Marionette Theatre. He is mesmerized and sells his school books for admission to the show. It's all beginning to sound terribly familiar! But thanks to the prompting of the blue-haired fairy, who tells Pinocchio that education is the means of his becoming a real boy, he does eventually get to school. There he commits to writing and arithmetic in the expectation that his new skills will enable him to buy Geppetto a warm woollen jacket with diamond buttons.

His immediate priority is 'to learn to read right away', but distractions still abound. The other boys mock him for being nerdy and paying too much attention to the teacher. They say that he talks 'like a printed book'. A fox and a cat warn him that going to school has left them blind and lame, and a friend called Lampwick tells him about Toyland, where everyone plays all day and no one works: 'There are no schools there; there are no teachers there; there are no books there. Now that's the sort of place that appeals to me!' Lampwick associates books with difficulty and Toyland is by far the better prospect. Pinocchio falls captive and they have a wonderful time in that magical place, until he wakes up in the morning with donkey ears. A squirrel informs him that boys who do nothing but play always grow into donkeys eventually. So it proves for our wayward wooden boy. Further misfortunes follow, but eventually there is an ending we can all applaud. He becomes a real boy at last, finds a bag of 40 freshly minted gold coins, is reunited with Geppetto, who has resumed his woodcarving career, and they live happily ever after.

Now let me tell you what Carlo Collodi, the author of the story, originally had in mind. Pinocchio's adventures began life in serial form in a Rome newspaper in 1881–82. Children loved them, and they were published in book form a year later. In the original serialized version, Pinocchio dies a terrible death – hanged for his repeated faults at the end of Chapter 15. At the request of his editor, however, Collodi added new chapters that made possible Pinocchio's rescue and eventual transformation into a real boy with a deeper understanding of himself. Of course I'm glad that the little rascal escapes the noose and lives his dream, but before we all rejoice or reach for the tissues ponder this. I've outlined the story as a reprimand to myself: I thought I knew it but the facts are otherwise. I had not really paid attention to the original and had settled instead for something 'seen through a glass darkly' – a sanitized and abridged film that left out or changed some of the most challenging and thoughtful passages of the book. Perhaps this has also been your experience in the light of these last paragraphs?

There is also the matter of Pinocchio's failures. These are many, but one in particular is easy to overlook. Although we are told that he does well at school and passes with high honours, despite his intention to learn to read at the first opportunity he doesn't become a serious reader. He never really grasps what it means 'to learn to read'. Recall for a moment that his classmates accuse him of speaking 'like a printed book'. In other words, he manages the first two steps of the learning ladder – the alphabet and the surface of a text. But there he stops. He does not see books as sources of revelation about his own experience and he never explores their deeper meanings. It's all surface work, mouthing slogans and sentences that convey messages rather than meaning. The various guides that he meets on his travels do little to further his deeper education. As his 'teachers' they fail to keep him company in his moments of darkness; even worse, they never help him to reflect on his own peculiar condition as a puppet with human aspirations or encourage him to explore what he means by his wish of 'becoming a boy'. All they offer is distraction and a contempt or derision for books and their hidden secrets. Pinocchio does not perish (at least not in the extended version of his adventures) as a result of such liaisons and bad advice, but he does pay a price that has contemporary significance:

> Pinocchio will only learn if he is not in a hurry to learn, and will only become a full individual through the effort required to learn slowly. Whether in Collodi's age of parroted school texts or in ours of almost infinite regurgitated facts available at our fingertips, it is relatively easy to be superficially literate . . . But to go further and deeper, to have the courage to face our fears and doubts . . . in order to learn and think, we need to learn to read in other ways differently. Pinocchio may turn into a boy at the conclusion of his adventures, but ultimately he still thinks like a puppet.[11]

I find real pathos in this summing up of Pinocchio's achievements – 'he still thinks like a puppet', despite the fact that in the book he looks upon the puppet he was with amused satisfaction. But I also recognize in this most fabulous and instructive story an incentive to exercise control and discipline over what I read: how, in other words, I derive meaning from the experience of finding uncommon or searching words on a page that in an earlier time Augustine might have kissed in his devotion as he imprinted them in his mind 'as on a wax tablet'.[12]

This image of a saint and scholar with a passion for words that appeared to him as real, burning presences and inspired his own poetic sensibilities suggests to me that our own distractions and weak wills (it's best to be honest about ourselves on this matter!) can be overcome when, like Augustine and teachers of wisdom before him, we learn something 'by heart'. Initially, this amounts to the practice of *stopping* – stop talking, stop surfing the internet, stop the mental fidgeting, stop expecting simple, immediate or easy answers and stop kneeling before the lure of the little red light that tells us we have a message on our phone (I've had three on mine as I've typed this sentence!) – in order to learn and remember texts that have the power to make us more human and that in time we may come to cherish.[13] What slow and serious reading can teach us is 'how to sit still for long periods and confront time head-on . . . so that we forget all of life's lesser woes and simply bask in the everlasting present'.[14] Reading comes pretty close to a religious experience at this level – in the same way that prayer, or for that matter poetry, calls for the attention or absorption that helps to banish the racing demons that hijack our consciousness.

Poetry can be a very good place to begin the difficult work of *stopping*. Lyrical poetry in particular requires only short periods of concentration. When it is read slowly, if possible aloud, we can find ourselves returning to a passage simply because we love it. It feeds us and affords us a deeper understanding. And the more we come back to it, the deeper the reward. There are always nagging questions, of course: isn't poetry difficult, or haven't we left the pursuit of this particular art form a little too late?

Edward Thomas is remembered and revered as one of the finest poets of the First World War. Before he was killed in 1917 in a shell explosion in the Arras offensive, he had written some of the best poems to come out of Britain at the beginning of the twentieth century. Just three years earlier he had felt that he 'couldn't write poetry to save my life' and confined himself to producing book reviews or travelogues, making restless journeys as he struggled to support a wife and three children and cope with bouts of frightening depression. A ray of light came unexpectedly when he visited a new bookshop whose main business was poetry. There he encountered the brilliant stars of literary London: the American Ezra Pound, who liked to greet startled guests at his flat in a flamboyant, purple dressing gown; W. B. Yeats, an Irish poet and playwright who still favoured candlelight instead of electricity for his evening readings; and Rupert Brooke, a debonair young English poet who would die a soldier in 1915, whose poetry sold 250,000 copies in the ten years following his death.

Thomas was neither particularly glamorous nor eccentric but he was open to persuasion. When he met Robert Frost – another American in London aiming to extend his reputation in a new country – Thomas acted on the advice of his 'Yankee' contemporary: 'Write poetry,' Frost suggested, 'and remember that words exist in the mouth and not in books.' Thomas was galvanized by this evocative image and also by the imminent prospect of war. The man who could not write a word of verse became a prolific poet. War concentrated his mind. One poem in particular, his beautiful 'Adlestrop', evokes the poignancy and atmosphere of that last summer before the monstrous sound of cannon fire utterly changed lives for ever.

> Yes, I remember Adlestrop –
> the name, because one afternoon
> of heat the express-train drew up there
> unwontedly. It was late June.
>
> The steam hissed. Someone cleared his throat.
> No one left and no one came
> on the bare platform. What I saw
> was Adlestrop – only the name
>
> And willows, willow-herb and grass,
> and meadowsweet, and haycocks dry,

no whit less still and lonely fair
than the high cloudlets in the sky.

And for that minute a blackbird sang
close by, and round him, mistier
farther and farther, all the birds
of Oxfordshire and Gloucestershire.

If we give it time, this is a poem that can provide the means of *stopping*, of providing respite for us on the hissing express and enfolding us in a quite unforced radiance of words. In four simple but profound verses we are both quietened and educated in the importance of the passing moment: the fleeting, precious seconds that will never return – 'and in that minute a blackbird sang' – and the soft, still landscape that will not be seen again. Four verses to which we can return with gratitude because they are written by a man in a hurry, who started late 'at 36 in the shade', who doubted his own ability to write or appreciate much beyond the prosaic or perfunctory, yet managed finally to sit still and chronicle the passage of time in words that cry out to be mouthed and remembered.

It's not too late to discover, or rediscover, the lure of poetry and it doesn't have to be recondite or arcane. Notice that I'm using two difficult words here to argue that poetry is not difficult! But you will agree, I hope, that they are lovely to mouth and linger over! If you still need convincing, let me give you one final example – this time an anonymous masterpiece that goes back at least to the sixteenth century:

O western wind, when wilt thou blow
That the small rain down can rain?
Christ, that my love were in my arms
And I in my bed again!

The verse amounts to a mere 130 characters. Why does it speak to me? It's raw, honest and human and saturated with the ache that epitomizes both the reality of absence and the desire, the deepest passionate desire of true love, that things should be otherwise. The name of Christ in this verse is uttered not as a profanity but as a form of beseeching that all lovers experience in times of separation or grief. In four lines we are exposed to an experience that chimes with our own desperate and confused longings and invites us to stop, think and, possibly, even pray.

Poetry testifies to depth – to bereavement and love, to suffering and joy. It can make of us serious or ethical readers who have come to know or want to believe that words have more to offer us than information or even consolation. Poetry represents 'a form of secular prayer and it's the point in language where one is most truthful ... when we want as writers and readers to speak our souls or our hearts'.[15] Poetry slows us down, forms part of the music of being properly human and helps us to bear witness in a way quite unknown to Pinocchio or his distracting entourage of unreflective puppets.

6

Wisdom and music

————◆◆◆————

'Without music, life would be a mistake.' The quotation comes from the philosopher Friedrich Nietzsche, who was exceedingly fond of aphorisms and grand statements. But in this instance and based on my own experience as an amateur music lover whose inner life has been profoundly influenced by musical experiences, I find myself in broad agreement with Nietzsche's sentiment. Music can and frequently does make a huge difference to our well-being and our capacity for joy and delight. It is also a cure for sadness and a help in trouble when life, hope or ambitions are threatened.

Writers, critics and thinkers have tried to define this power. The poet Rilke called it 'the breathing of statues' – an evocative image that takes us deeper into the mystery of music. Less reverently, George Bernard Shaw described it as 'the brandy of the damned'. Perhaps he had the Talmud in mind here, where we learn that Solomon, the wisest of men, fell into the worship of idols by the music of a thousand instruments brought to him by the daughters of Pharaoh.

I'm not sure that definitions help us very much, however, as I find it difficult to articulate the connection between music and the world. Musical meaning is elusive, forever changing and, for most of us, deeply personal. What delights one listener leaves another unmoved, or perhaps horrified. Many parents enduring the sound of their teenager's latest acquisition being played at maximum volume in the bedroom will testify to this truth! Add to this common experience the profusion of forms that music takes – pop, folk, rock, hip-hop, heavy metal, classical, country and jazz – and we are soon forced to concede that any definition is going to fall short. Music is as vast, complex and protean as the world itself and all we really know is how impoverished our lives would be without it. As the jazz legend Duke Ellington tells us, 'There are two kinds of music: music that sounds good and whatever you want to call that other stuff.'

What I'm after in this chapter is the 'good stuff' – the music that can nourish our lives, expose us to deeper truths, increase our human sympathies and open our minds and hearts to the mysterious and sublime. My choices are personal and eclectic but in my experience they have come to represent a form of wisdom bought at a price. By this I mean that listening to music is not a passive activity like getting a haircut or buying a burger at the drive-through. It is something for us to *do*. Like any worthwhile or exacting endeavour, music makes demands, and what it can offer us will generally be in proportion to what we ourselves are prepared to give. In her fascinating memoir *The Spiral Staircase*, the theologian and former nun Karen Armstrong reminds us that in the matter of prayer, 'you have to give it your full attention, wait patiently upon it, and make an empty space for it in your mind'.[1] An apt formulation for music too, once we experience its potency to fashion our responses to the world in new or unexpected ways.

Just two examples to make the point. The renowned cellist Pablo Casals was surrounded by music from infancy but at the age of 11 heard the cello for the first time. He had never seen one before and when he heard the first notes he felt as if he could not breathe, such was the beauty of its sound. For the next 80 years and more he 'was wedded to the instrument' and his playing represented his 'salute to life'.[2] For Casals, music was not simply a matter of pleasure in creating but rather a personal testimony to his belief that he had been graced with a rare gift that he had a duty to cherish and share.

From a different place and time another boy, again aged 11, comes into view. One day he will become a notable critic and writer on classical music, but as we see him now he is standing outside a dingy Cambridge cinema. It's 1940 and he is about to experience something akin to first love through hearing the fabulous soundtrack of Disney's *Fantasia*. A great film, but what brings him back after school each day to stand undisturbed in a quiet alley outside the cinema is the music of Leopold Stokowski and the Philadelphia Orchestra playing Bach, Beethoven, Schubert and Stravinsky. Music will become his life's work, frequently stopping his breath, unsettling his heart and eventually leading him to Mozart, whose work encompasses everything – love, lost love, joy, death, desire and forgiveness – 'without heroics, with delicious wit, and with an unruffled sense of beauty'.[3]

Both stories appeal to me but I identify more closely with the second. By the age of 11 I had been a church chorister for three years. I can't claim a comparable moment of epiphany but rehearsing and singing the psalms each week began to affect me and fired my imagination. Dedicated choir masters instilled in me a respect for the sound of words and the serenity and pathos of particular hymns. I became fascinated with, and not a little fearful of, an unknown region to which they seemed to point – somewhere otherworldly and spacious. I sang the words, 'Let all mortal flesh keep silence and in fear and trembling stand', and without knowing exactly why it moved me, I knew I was immersed in something vast. The echo of an anthem dying away had the same effect, evoking in my mind spacious and ethereal images of the purest light.

Childhood gave way to adolescence and a few years later I discovered The Beatles, The Rolling Stones and The Who as they defined and delighted my generation. In the USA and Canada, the folk singers Joni Mitchell, Joan Baez and Judy Collins crafted songs of love and peace. Bob Dylan testified that the times were changing. The lovely harmonies of the Mamas and Papas and the Beach Boys came out of California, and the coming age of Aquarius was celebrated in the unconstrained vibrancy of the musical *Hair*. Everything seemed possible, but we were wrong.

On 21 August 1968, just one night after Communist troops had invaded Czechoslovakia, the Soviet Union Symphony

Orchestra performed a programme at the London Proms that included Antonín Dvořák's Cello Concerto. The audience booed to register its protest at the illegal act of invasion, but tears followed as the Russian cellist Mstislav Rostropovich transformed the composition into a lament for an event that neither he nor the orchestra had been aware of until one of its players had tuned in to a pirate radio station.

That particular concert, aided by the imaginative genius of Rostropovich, demonstrated the power of music that helps us negotiate our lives and the issues we face as human beings. The contemporary American composer John Adams, who has written music to commemorate the 9/11 terrorist attacks in New York, found his texts in unexpected places: in the brief phone calls to loved ones from victims caught in the planes and buildings that dreadful day, and in the obituaries that ran daily in the *New York Times* for almost a year after the events. His choral work *On the Transmigration of Souls* was first performed on 19 September 2002. Adams described it as a memory space for those who had been left to mourn and an opportunity for them to be alone with their thoughts and emotions. On hearing the work for the first time, one seasoned concert-goer described the music as the most moving thing he had ever heard in a concert hall. At the time Adams spoke of his concern and duty as a composer to bring listeners to a place where music is able to satisfy inarticulate longings and the deepest feelings:

> It's not my intention to attempt 'healing' in this piece. The event will always be there in memory, and the lives of those who suffered will forever remain burdened by the violence and the pain. Instead, the best I can hope for is to create something that has both the serenity and the kind of gravitas that old cathedrals possess . . . We have learned all too well how to keep our emotions in check, and we know how to mask them with humour or irony. Music has a singular capacity to unlock those controls and bring us face to face with our raw, uncensored, unattenuated feelings.[4]

Adams's insight resonates with my own experience and reflects one of the reasons why I continue to hold on to and cherish my back catalogue of rock music – the conviction I share with others that music is 'a storm on the senses, weather for the soul, deeper than deep, wider than wide'.[5] In short, it is not something to be trifled with and possesses something of the oceanic.

I was fortunate to live through a revolutionary era, but after the ground-breaking albums and protest songs of those remarkable years another kind of upheaval took place in my head. I can't name a date but I recall standing at a bus stop hugging an LP of Tchaikovsky's Sixth Symphony, quite unable to believe that I had acquired this astonishingly assured and creative masterpiece for 50 pence! I listened to it in darkness, memorized its movements, read about Tchaikovsky's troubled life and began to understand why his musical patron, Madame Nadezhda von Meck, who supported him financially for 13 years, felt that she could die experiencing his music. It embraces a particular world of yearning and desire, of suffering, loss and resignation. But I clapped my hands chiefly because it was, and is, simply beautiful in its pathos and silence, its passion and exuberance. This was music tracing the change and upheavals of my own life, speaking to my felt experience but also opening for me a portal to a parallel world. A largely unknown cosmos produced by instruments and the human voice, touching our roots and remembered past, affirming life in all its strange complexity and translating feelings of joy, hope and sadness into symphonies and songs of love, travel and farewell.

So began an exploration that has never stopped. Unsurprisingly, perhaps, I have developed a deep love of church music – in particular composers of the late Renaissance such as Gibbons and Byrd, and the 40-part motet *Spem in alium* ('Hope in any other') by Thomas Tallis. There is a timelessness in their compositions that transcended 'the narrow bound of their origins and spoke to new generations in new places'.[6] I discovered the lyricism and elegiac sweep of Elgar's music and read of the famed conductor who made the sign of the cross before the start of the slow movement of that composer's First Symphony. Elgar led me to the mysticism of Vaughan Williams – a deeply humane composer troubled by doubts whose contribution to the liturgical life of the Church has been immense. I have a particular day in mind when I was unable to hold back tears as his *Five Variants of Dives and Lazarus* for harp and string orchestra formed the backcloth to a dance sequence in Canterbury Cathedral. The energy and inventiveness of William Walton thrilled and surprised me – in particular, the atmospheric pressure of his First Symphony and the breathtaking rendition of the biblical texts that form his cantata *Belshazzar's Feast*, first performed at the Leeds Festival in 1931. It remains a thrilling experience for the first-time listener today with its drama and poignancy. A dear friend introduced me to Wagner: I went to the opera for the first time, spending almost eight hours in the Palace Theatre Manchester one Saturday afternoon and evening as *The Twilight of the Gods*, the concluding (and epic) part of his Ring cycle, pummelled the audience into submission and, finally, silence. A boxed set of Brahms's symphonies conducted by Herbert von Karajan became a prized possession, and a bust of Beethoven found a permanent place in a special corner of the living room. Johann Sebastian Bach, however, came to surpass them both in importance.

Like many people, I had perhaps a dim awareness that Bach's *St Matthew Passion* represented one of the greatest musical achievements ever. I did not know that it had fallen on deaf ears when it was first performed in Leipzig in 1727, and that some 18 months later his employers at St Thomas's Church and school decided by seven votes to four to reduce his salary. Bach remonstrated, but to no avail; he remained in Leipzig for the remaining 20 years of his life. God had called him to be cantor and director of music there, and with God's help he had to endure the local intrigues and quarrels, financial worries, the unrelenting slog of work and the ingratitude of a city council that did not have a high opinion of him: they had originally preferred another musician for the post. The council meeting minutes for April 1723 record: 'Since we cannot get the best man, we must put up with a mediocre one.'[7] With hindsight they would surely have read: 'We failed to get the best man but we gained a genius instead.'

The more I have listened to Bach over the years – and for a long time I played one of his cantatas every Sunday morning in my study to prepare for worship – the more convinced I have become of his extraordinary creativity and faith. His music is dedicated to God, and whether it is the piercing notes of the trumpets in the final 'Grant us thy peace' of the *B Minor Mass* or the quiet but thrilling sounds of his Advent compositions, he points us beyond the music to the ground and source of all things – the Creator and Judge who sets our lives and deaths within a providential order. We listen to Bach and we learn of the faith of Luther and the German Reformation – that God is a safe stronghold, is at all times to be trusted, and for all our failings is merciful and good.

We can also hear the music of the great German organist and composer Dietrich Buxtehude: as a young man of 20, Bach was so inspired by this towering figure that he took four weeks off work and walked the 250 miles from Arnstadt to Lübeck (with perhaps a few lifts on the way!) to hear Buxtehude conduct the famous *Evening Music* in St Mary's Church. The church was packed as the orchestra and choir related the age-old story of Good and Evil, of Heaven and Hell, with the intense devotion that was to define Bach's later choral masterpieces.

In Bach's living and dying we come to see that great things can be achieved despite the many petty hindrances and limitations that make up our less brilliant days. He encourages us to persevere, and not take ourselves too seriously. On one occasion, after being complimented on his wonderful organ playing, he said, 'There's nothing wonderful about it: you just put down the right notes and the organ does the rest!'[8] The lack of pomposity is endearing, as is his accepting attitude towards his death. At the end of his life, following an unsuccessful operation on his eyes that left him tired and eventually blind, he dictated the last of 18 chorale preludes to his son-in-law and asked that it should be given the title, 'I come before thy throne of grace.' He died a few days later in his sixty-sixth year, a pilgrim to the end with no apparent fear of death,[9] a watchman ever mindful of the city of God and the sound of harpists singing a new song before his throne (Rev. 14.3), and a teacher whose music elevates and never disappoints.[10]

At this point I'm trying to resist the temptation to continue naming the composers who have enlarged my understanding and nourished my mind and heart. I am indebted to the symphonies of Sibelius and Nielsen and their exhilarating affirmations of the human spirit; to the music of Janáček which taught me that love can be found again, even in old age; to Fauré for the gentle peace of his *Requiem*; to Samuel Barber for his *Adagio for Strings* that always speaks to me of bare trees against a clear winter sky; and to Messiaen for his compositions that incorporate birdsong as a symbol of the resurrected soul in flight.

There is one man, however, a Jewish musician from a land without a name, who has exerted a particular influence on me for the greater part of my life. At times his music has served as a personal refuge; on other occasions as a guide, as it prompts what Milton described as 'those thoughts that wander through eternity'.[11] I was lent the symphonies of Gustav Mahler in my early twenties. I listened dutifully before returning them, unaware that I was not ready for their scope or ambition, and ignorant of the facts of Mahler's life. I had not grasped that before me was a composer who wished his music to embrace the whole world and the deepest questions of the heart. A man whose father ran a tavern in the town of Iglau on the border of Bohemia and Moravia and whose mother gave birth to 14 children, a Jew who abandoned his Judaism and converted to

Catholicism in order to assume the directorship of the Vienna Court Opera in 1897, Mahler was a complex individual who thought too much and felt everything intensely. He was a restless soul, obsessed by death and mortality, who saw seven of his siblings die in infancy and lost his own daughter Maria in 1907 when she was four. A sense of the tragic was never far from his experience, yet in his music there is a world of honesty free from pettiness, ravishing testimonies to the beauty of nature – 'the beloved earth blossoms everywhere in Spring and turns green again'[12] – and deeply felt genuflections to love. Many familiar with the beautiful *Adagietto* of the Fifth Symphony may not be aware that it represents a love letter to his wife Alma, a musical eternity ring implying love until death.

Above all, Mahler offers us vistas beyond this world, especially in his Second and Eighth Symphonies. In 2011 I fulfilled a long-standing ambition to sing in the vast choir required for the Eighth (often called the *Symphony of a Thousand*). After many weeks of rehearsals, combined choirs gathered in Liverpool's Anglican cathedral for what proved to be a quite overwhelming experience. The same kind of feeling comes to mind as I think of the first time that I attended a performance of the Second (*The Resurrection*) at the Free Trade Hall in Manchester, more than 30 years ago.

The Second Symphony is a transfiguring experience. To Mahler it sounded 'as if it came from some other world . . . one is battered to the ground and then raised on angels' wings to the highest heights'.[13] On hearing the symphony in the Vatican in January 2004, Pope John Paul spoke of its quest for 'a sincere reconciliation among all believers in one God'.[14] The work is certainly ecumenical in the broadest sense and as it comes to a searing conclusion it affirms that it is not only the righteous who will rise again. Describing the finale, Mahler wrote: 'The glory of God appears. A wondrous light strikes us to the heart. All is quiet and blissful. Behold: there is no judgement, no sinner, no just man, no great and small; there is no punishment, no

reward. An overwhelming love . . .'[15] Mahler is staking everything on a God who brings back *all* the dead. He remembers
the early prayers he would have learned as a boy from his
teacher, Rabbi Unger, composed five centuries before Christ,
that testify to a King who 'keeps His faith with those who sleep
in the dust'. And he is challenging all who are listening, or
performing, to think again about the scope of divine love and
the fullest, truest meaning of resurrection.

Mahler himself left this world on 18 May 1911, following an
incurable heart infection, dying in Vienna aged 50. While he is
on his deathbed, his wife Alma, who a year earlier had started
a torrid affair with the architect Walter Gropius, looks on as
he tells their little daughter Anna to be good; his body is washed
in preparation for what will follow. Two attendants lift him from
the bed and the scene appears to onlookers as a 'taking down
from the cross'. Four days later he is buried in Grinzing cemetery.
Under a threatening sky, a priest recites words of commenda-
tion and a crowd of many hundreds stands silent as the coffin
is lowered into the grave. At that moment the rain ceases and
a nightingale's song is heard over the silence, an intimation
perhaps of his Second Symphony, where a lonely bird, the last
in all creation, soars aloft, free of all terror and sadness.

Only a month before this, Mahler had been in New York, where
for three years he delighted audiences and inspired orchestras
and singers under his baton. His influence endured long after
his death; when the great conductor Leonard Bernstein died in
1990, he was buried with the score of Mahler's Fifth Symphony
placed over his heart.

It was a particular privilege and pleasure for me to be able
to preach a sermon in that city on the centenary of Mahler's
death and to remind my congregation of a conductor and composer who lived several lives in what we would regard today as
a relatively short span. I spoke of his resilience and energy, his
commitment to artistic excellence, his boundless curiosity, his
quest for love and his refusal to accept defeat. I also told them

of his immortal longings – the sense he had so long before his death of having left the world behind, and the music he wrote to convey this truth. One song in particular, 'Ich bin der Welt abhanden gekommen' ('I am lost to the world'), illustrates this with an unsurpassed ache and purity. Mahler offers us what feels like a single moment in time, a snapshot among fleeting moments, yet in this moment there is an undeniable intimation of otherness – a beyond in our midst where 'we are at peace in a still stretch of land'.[16]

It is not surprising to learn that lives other than my own are changed by this demanding composer and his inimitable and sometimes difficult artistic creations. But in his magnificence and all too evident human frailty and foibles, he takes us to his real and imagined worlds, invites us to ponder the brevity and joy of life, and teaches us that its struggles are worthwhile.

I suspect that it's more than coincidence that my two greatest Mahler experiences were shared with others in a great cathedral and a concert hall. To be part of a huge choir in a building consecrated to the glory of a transcendent God, or an audience completely absorbed by a symphony that speaks of ultimate things, is to experience the unifying power of music as it mediates truth and goodness and exposes us to the beauty that creates a new sort of communion with the turning world. We come to understand (if only fleetingly) what the great religions mean by the idea of grace – 'that God's relation to the world as a whole, and to each of us in particular, is one of giving'.[17] Music corroborates the sense that believers have, that the world is sustained by gift, that all sacred moments are gift – 'of gift revealed as *the way things are*'.[18] It explains Pablo Casals' 'salute to life', and why the best musicians continue to view their work in terms of a vocation – of repaying life its favours. Music, in the forms I have described in this chapter,[19] approximates to a kind of divine disclosure that invites us to trust and obey the One who is the source of all good things. It tells us that we can learn to love the world unconditionally, with all its ragged edges and deformities, because it is loved by God. And it offers us the wisdom more precious than pearls – that to be spiritual is not to cultivate a private place of comfort from the storm. It is instead that particular form of attention that enables us to become the music, to share in the dance that is the energy of God flowing through creation, to receive only to give, and in giving to receive again.

I began this chapter with the admission that in my own experience music is a generous but assertive partner. Let me say a little more: or better still, let a musician say it for me! In the words of violinist Rose Mary Harbison:

> Music requires from us . . . a willingness to probe its rich intricacies, the capacity to be startled and dismayed, to have one's soul tormented a little, to come unadorned, emotionally fresh, to stand along with others and witness the hopes and the vision of the composer.[20]

Such an attitude or disposition calls for a respect for music and for those who make it that borders on reverence. We are on holy ground. Clean ears are required, along with preparation and the readiness not only to enjoy the music for the beauty or delight it affords but to engage with the composer's life, ideas, struggles and beliefs. As the final movement of Mahler's Ninth Symphony dissolves into silence, I too am silent. I am conscious of a man who in this work faces his demons and seeks to transcend them, and in so doing speaks to our own fragile hopes, grief and loss. I know that much, maybe even all, of what I'm suggesting here will annoy or baffle those who want their music like their coffee – quick and ready to go. That's fine, and actually it's fine for me too on days when nothing more than easy listening is needed. But it belongs to another category: it's not the 'good stuff', which demands more of our attention and satisfies at a quite different level; the music that appeals to the 'better angels of our nature',[21] and opens the secret door to the wisdom we never knew existed.

7

Wisdom and the emotions

One of the most familiar and loved Communion prayers begins with the words 'Almighty God, to whom all hearts are open, all desires known, and from whom no secrets are hidden . . .' I love the opening for its subtlety, its depth and insight. It's not quite a confession – that comes a little later in the service – but represents instead the ready admission that God knows how things are with us and that this fact is both alarming and liberating. The writer and feminist Janet Morley describes this in terms of 'an appalled sense of self-exposure combined with a curious but profound relief'.[1]

The Christian way calls for the integration of our personal desires, and each act of worship entails an offering of ourselves in the humbling but gratifying knowledge that we are accepted. What I find interesting is that the prayer takes our desires and therefore our emotions seriously. Together they constitute a huge and significant dimension of what it means to be human. In relation to living wisely and well, it matters that we try to be logical and reasonable, perhaps even given to the life of the mind or the pursuit of the coolness and balm that lies at the heart of one of our most cherished hymns.[2] But there is more to us than this. In holding on to our brains and the belief that reason is a good and necessary thing, we must also acknowledge that we are creatures characterized by deep feelings and volcanic emotions that can shock or surprise us. Such responses, sometimes predictable, on other occasions overwhelming and unexpected, can be a source of wisdom offering important insights into the geography of the emotional life and how it contributes

90

to our well-being and moral imagination. Part of our religious vocation is to be good, even holy (Lev. 11.44–45; 1 Pet. 1.16). That we frequently fail in this endeavour may be due to a deeper failure on our part to recognize or acknowledge that we do indeed contain immensities – powerful impulses and con-tradictions that shape our identity and what we might become.

Emotions are slippery things and can easily be confused with related experiences such as moods and appetites. But a definition is possible. We are talking about love, hate, delight, shame, disgust, anger, envy, grief, jealousy, joy, suffering, pride and astonishment. An impressive if somewhat daunting cata-logue! This list is not exhaustive: it does not include more complex emotions such as, for example, the incipient fear of death that insinuates itself into the fabric of most lives and accounts for many of our actions and responses; or the repressed resentment of a loved one or friend that might be expressed through depression or passive anger.

The Gospels are littered with such instances. Quite apart from the light they shine on Jesus, this helps to explain their endur-ing appeal to many who are not conventionally religious but are fascinated by these compelling narratives that show us at our best and worst.[3] Judas, for example, still haunts our collective imagination – we feel his rage, his calculations and his remorse, and no contemporary presentation of the Passion works without his brooding presence. Mary, the mother of Jesus, speaks to us in her fierce yet silent grief as she stands at the foot of the cross, reminding every parent that the depth of love is always measured in loss. And the indifference or contempt of the watching crowd as the Son of God is erased from the earth tells us something disquieting about the fickleness of the human heart – even in the presence of the purest love.

The claim being advanced is that the emotions involve import-ant things – the responses and judgements we make that mould our character and the recognition of our human limitations as we confront experiences that we do not or cannot fully control.

Before I share two stories involving complex and intense emotions that support my argument, a couple of caveats need to be addressed. Two generations ago, most psychologists were not inclined to view the inner world of experience as germane to their work. Emotions were destined to disappear from the remit of science as relics of a pre-scientific past – vague, unobservable and impossible to measure: 'Why introduce ... an unneeded term such as emotion, when there are already scientific terms for everything we have to describe?'[4] Such statements were common until the 1950s but eventually proved unfounded.

In recent years, the disciplines of psychology and philosophy have paid increasing attention to the emotions as significant indicators concerning the ways in which humans and other animals perceive and interpret the world. In a similar way, we can detect in the teachings of the Church, particularly in the formative centuries of Christianity and the writings of Augustine, a suspicion that the emotions belonged to that category of human experience that takes us away from God and hinders the ascent of the soul as it climbs the ladder of perfection. Thankfully (and this is not always understood or appreciated in readings of his work), Augustine had second thoughts and came to recognize the validity of the emotions that characterized the virtuous lives of followers of Jesus such as Paul – and, in particular, Jesus himself, his crucified Lord, who was really human and really suffered in a human body. Augustine saw that although emotions can mislead and even manipulate us in harmful ways, no genuinely good life is possible without them. Our ascent to God necessarily takes place within our humanity and our human and Christian emotions represent two parts of the same story. A genuine love of God is characterized not simply by the intellect but by longing, desire, and a sense of incompleteness or restlessness that can never be satisfied until we finally rest in the divine physician – God alone: 'When I shall be united to you in every part of myself, there will be for me no more sorrow or toil, and my life will be alive, in every way full of you.'[5]

Augustine is all future tense here, employing a language predicated on the vision of God and a City beyond the cares and distractions of this world. But we should remember that prior to his conversion he was well acquainted with the taste of a lover's body and, following the death of his son, the grief that feels like a cul-de-sac or an amputation. He would instinctively, I believe, grasp the depth and significance of the following two stories.

The first concerns a distinguished American academic, Martha C. Nussbaum, Professor of Law and Ethics at the University of Chicago. In April 1992 she travelled to Trinity College, Dublin to give a lecture. Her mother was in hospital in Philadelphia, recovering from a serious but routine operation. Complications developed unexpectedly, however, and her life was in danger. The professor was notified and arrangements were made for her to return on the first available flight. She fulfilled the speaking engagement, not as an eminent philosopher entirely at ease with her subject but as 'a person invaded by the world, barely containing tears'.[6] Later, as she tried to sleep, her mother appeared to her in a dream. She was smiling and looked young and beautiful, just as Nussbaum remembered her from her own childhood. As she travelled back on the transatlantic flight the next day, she tried to retain this image of hope but her body interposed. Her hands began to shake and she experienced a deep anger towards the flight attendants for smiling as if everything was under control and herself for not having been present when the crisis occurred. Arriving in Philadelphia, the nurse on duty in the hospital intensive care unit informed her that her mother had died just 20 minutes earlier. She was lying on the bed, in her best dressing gown and impeccably made-up – the staff knew that she always liked her lipstick on straight. The sight reduced Nussbaum to tears and she wept uncontrollably. She was offered a glass of water, and just an hour later she was on her way to a hotel in a hospital van, carrying her mother's overnight bag containing clothes and books – the poignant artefacts of a life that no longer belonged to this world.

In the weeks that followed, the professor noticed several things: periods of weeping combined with fatigue, and nightmares in which she felt vulnerable and alone as a strange animal seemed to walk across her bed; a resurgent anger directed towards the nurses for not prolonging her mother's life until she arrived and the doctors for allowing a straightforward medical procedure to go wrong; and anger at herself – her demanding career and high commitment to work had inevitably made less time available for her mother. However, her professional activities, combined with the normal events and responsibilities of daily life made her grief less traumatic than the emotional turmoil experienced by her sister, who had lived near to their mother and visited most days. They had loved her equally but the nature of their respective lives and duties affected the duration of their emotional upheaval. On the other hand, Nussbaum recognized that although her current life was less disrupted in the aftermath of her mother's death, she experienced the 'odd sensation of having been robbed of a history, of being no longer a person who had a family history'.[7] In relation to this, the appearance of Nussbaum's former husband at the funeral service gave her an unexpected joy; through his presence she was to see in him 20 years of life with her mother: a shared past lived again. That she had been able to give a speech on behalf of the family also made her feel less helpless, although even this achievement made her question how much she had really loved her mother, when she had spoken with such smooth assurance.

I've gone back to this story several times in recent years and I can recall its impact on first reading. It's a human story that will resonate with many readers acquainted with some of the conflicting emotions that attend any genuine grief. It also raises important issues concerning self-awareness, as we see a normally cool and composed individual succumb to a tangle of emotional complexities. Writing here as a husband and father rather than a priest or theologian, I am aware that Nussbaum's experience takes me back to a hospital more than 30 years ago.

After waiting for a long time in some anguish, I was led into an ante-room by a nurse to be told that my newly born daughter had died. Apart from some tears as I held her a few minutes later, I was able to talk with my wife and hospital staff, drive home, perform routine domestic chores and inform our neighbours. Later my priest colleague called at the house, and as he put his arms around me I disintegrated.

Times change, and in a contemporary culture that has become suspicious of physical gestures that may be deemed 'inappropriate', I note that I was held in my grief by another – by a man who knew that tears and emotions constituted the proper business of the Church and responded accordingly. I have not forgotten this. Nussbaum, you will remember, was offered nothing more than a glass of water as she wept and began to lose control. This was presumably a professional response on the part of the nurses, dictated by patient–staff protocols. What it lacked, in my view, was the empathy and compassion that are called for as we stand alongside others in their unexpected sorrow. The gospel does require us to give water – but specifically to the thirsty. For those devastated by the shock of sudden death, something physical, humane and Christ-like may be required: a touch, a look or a gesture that testifies to human solidarity and religious concern in the face of loss, and an informed understanding of the disorderly operations of the emotions in our daily lives.

With regard to the latter, Nussbaum found enlightenment in the messy materials of grief. By the time she came to write about her mother's death, almost ten years after the event, she felt able to set down features of the emotions that contribute to our human flourishing. She had experienced their urgency and their heat, their tendency to take over the personality, sometimes with overwhelming force. She had noted their connection to things of ultimate importance – the life of a loved one in this instance – through which we define our own significance and worth. She had also registered their resistance to the rationality that was such an integral part of her teaching, writing and academic research, and how closely one emotion shaded into another. Hope alternated uneasily with fear before being dashed by grief. Grief then looked for a cause and expressed itself in anger. All these indicated an underlying love and displayed a dynamic relationship to one another. In recording her story and reflecting on it, Nussbaum shows us that we are often in the hands of the world when we choose to love: that we cannot admit some emotions while refusing others, once we allow an object beyond ourselves – in this case her mother – to lay claim to that which is deepest and, possibly, best in us.

Her insights are of real value and are underpinned by the wisdom of the ancients. Think, for example, of the Stoic philosopher Seneca,[8] who compared the emotions to fire or the dangerous currents of the sea or fierce gales. Before them we can feel passive or powerless. And that's the point – we often are. We are significantly disposed to believing that, appearances to the contrary, the world is the way that it should be, and often use one trick or another to convince ourselves that it is. Things are presumed to be orderly and reason reigns.[9] Our emotions, however, point to a different conclusion: the paradox that our frustrations rise with our expectations as we see and feel all too painfully that nature includes locusts, floods and lice as well as the grazing sheep and spacious meadows that speak of an Almighty hand. Like innocent and virtuous Job in the Bible, when his cattle and children are suddenly taken from him and his initial dignity and calm give way to howling and protest, our own vales of tears will sometimes reveal that we too are bodies as well as souls, bundles of fears, rages and longings, as we are tossed about and no longer masters of our world.

But this much we do come to know: that we are also in such circumstances often strangely alive, in fact intensely so; that certain things – a belief or cause, a principle or pursuit, another person – matter deeply to us, and that we would not feel so frustrated, resentful, broken or sad if they did not; that our anger or shame finds us out and tells us who we really are;

that our sorrows are a mere reflection of the greater, universal sorrows of Jobs without number in all ages. In our actual experience, we discover that reason, though much to be prized, plays only a modest part in our motivation. We are moved by desires and fears, passions and impulses, that effortlessly insinuate their way into our conscious behaviour and calculations. The great English philosopher Thomas Hobbes erected an entire political ideology on the bedrock of terror[10] and 'the war of all against all', but he also noted that he was born prematurely during a thunderstorm and 'his Mother dear, did bring forth twins, both me and fear'. The candour of this quotation tells us that Hobbes acknowledged the subterranean element in his philosophical masterpiece, *Leviathan*. A political theorist of genius, he was also a vulnerable human being, limited by his fearful beginnings and therefore possibly blind to ways of ordering society other than by force or contract.

Two stories were promised earlier – this is the second. In its intensity it stands comparison with Nussbaum's recollections, but introduces some new elements. Instead of an American academic of middle years, here is a philosopher recalling his younger self. He is a young man, aged 18, a seminarian training for the priesthood about to make an encounter with unexpected consequences:

> One day a girl came to the seminary with her father, who was there on some business with the Rector. She stood by the open door of the car, talking to some of the other seminarians. She was about twenty and pretty; graceful body, amused intelligent face, and I was standing in my cassock about fifteen yards away ... Suddenly the sight of her was quite unbearable and I was compelled to rush away to my room where I lay on my bed in agony and could face no one until well after I knew she was gone.[11]

A cursory reading of this account will take it to be about adolescent awkwardness and the assertion of sexual desire. Not so. Reflecting on this experience many years later and having jettisoned some of his earlier beliefs and priestly aspirations, the writer tells us that he became conscious of how little of the *physical power* of his feelings was captured by his recollection of the meeting. The fact that he felt unable to see people in the aftermath was surpassed by his physical weakness: 'there wasn't any strength in my limbs and to proceed was against the force of gravity'.[12] The sight of the girl induced a pain that he could make no sense of and could not be reduced to a sexual fantasy – 'I was much too disturbed for that'.[13] Confronted by innocence, youth and beauty in a particularly striking way, his energies deserted him; in the words of the Psalmist, he became as a man without strength (Ps. 88.4). A meeting with his Buddhist teacher for the first time had a similar effect: 'I had to walk through the physical aspect of my fear as though through a swamp to approach him.'[14]

What interests me about both incidents – in fact, what unites them – is the absence of energy: its depletion or inhibition that leaves him spent and vulnerable. Conversely, he is able to recall other moments where the sound of a bird or the sight of a tree produces in him a state of joy and he stands transfixed, feeling like a loaded gun. His energy becomes a source of wonder and all his strength and sweetness are 'rolled up into one ball'.[15] What he invariably feels in his body is the ebb and flow of energy, its release and repression, and an accompanying awareness of being either at its mercy or in command of it. What he also comes to recognize is that such energy as a strong physical dimension of the emotions can be a unifying force once its presence is acknowledged and integrated into our lives in an orderly way.

I hesitated before using the word 'orderly'. It has so many negative connotations in relation to the body and its inclinations, and religion has frequently failed to be a good teacher in this contested arena. Five years before his sighting of the young girl at the seminary, the writer had on frequent occasions made his confession in what he describes as a state of 'singular Catholic terror'.[16] He is on the cusp of adolescence and his sexual awakening – new sensations, whether involuntary or sought – trouble him and the gloomy conviction arises in his mind that he is committing a mortal sin. In the confessional box he blurts out something about personal impurity, touching and pollution (the conditioned responses he has been taught) and reels under the priestly reprimand that if he does not stop *now* he will be playing with himself on his deathbed.[17] Such an instruction hardly deserves the epithet 'orderly' and belongs instead to a familiar and depressing catalogue of Christian sexual ethics that has routinely outlawed the body and insisted on temperance, continence and rigid self-control or denial as the only means of mastering its drives. By contrast, what I have in mind is something more liberating and joyful – 'orderly' in the sense that the body and its disparate energies are affirmed and celebrated in terms of their sensitivity and their responses to the stimuli of an intoxicating world and novel experiences, but also marshalled in such a way that corrosive emotions such as needless or excessive anger or mad lust are prevented from laying waste to our lives.

Do you remember the story of Sinbad the sailor and how he tricks the genie? Sinbad opens the bottle and out comes a gigantic genie with the power to kill him outright. Clever Sinbad appeals to his vanity and wagers that he can't get back in the bottle. The genie has to prove him wrong, but as soon as he does so Sinbad puts the stopper back in the neck of the bottle until the genie learns to behave himself. Sometimes anger or lust can threaten us and others. We can't negotiate with such inflamed emotions until we have taught them a basic moral etiquette – which, following Sinbad, means putting them back in the bottle to demonstrate who is really in charge.[18] 'Orderly', on this view, is neither absolute censure nor denial, but is instead a form of containment when such action is called for, while being on other occasions an affirmation that sensuality can be wedded to the spirit as a means of our flourishing and how we are constituted as persons.

Key to this particular way of being in the world – what I have chosen to call the path of 'a spiritualized sensuality'[19] – is a deeper appreciation of the correlation between energy and our emotions referred to earlier. Science can tell us a lot concerning how emotions have their origins in the brain and, even more pertinently, how 'an intricate tapestry of chemical and electrical signals govern every thought and action'.[20] Energy courses through us, shaping our feelings and the basis of our personalities and the idea of 'the body electric' is now part of received wisdom in understanding what makes us human.

We have a poet, not a scientist, to thank for such an influential and allusive notion. Walt Whitman, the pivotal American poet of the nineteenth century, emerged from the family of a Long Island Quaker carpenter. After little by way of formal schooling, he followed a career in journalism, residing in Manhattan until his father's illness and subsequent death brought him back home in 1854. In the following ten years he began to be recognized as a poet of startling originality and a religious prophet with a unique grasp of himself, his age and his nation. During the Civil War he served as a volunteer nurse and wound-dresser in the military hospitals of Washington, DC. He excelled in these roles, and also collected money to buy pencils and paper, clothes, and brandy and ice cream for the wounded and often illiterate soldiers. He read letters from home to them, wrote notes on their behalf and comforted the suffering and dying.

No other writer or poet of his eminence did such laudable things or chronicle such terrible scenes.[21] Despite the appalling injuries he witnessed, he remained an ecstatic and sometimes elegiac chronicler of the self, rejoicing in the fleshliness of his being and seeking through it a reconciliation with his soul. As a poet who was disinclined to make any sharp distinction between thought and feeling or the human and divine – 'I can comprehend no being more wonderful than man'[22] – Whitman saw God incarnating himself in man: not just in Jesus, but in every person who went forth into the world singing his songs.[23] True to such convictions, he sang of 'the body electric' in his most celebrated work.[24] Too long to include in full here, I can at least offer a few lines from his work 'Song of Myself' that capture some of his genius and his 'spiritualized sensuality'. Read them slowly – better still, read them aloud, but quietly – and ponder how the son of a carpenter from Long Island anticipates the discoveries of science in a later age:

> Clear and sweet is my soul, and clear and sweet is all
>   that is not my soul.
> I am silent, and go bathe and admire myself.
> Welcome is every organ and attribute of me, and of any
>   man hearty and clean.
> Not an inch, not a particle of an inch is vile, and none
>   shall be less familiar than the rest.
> Mine is no callous shell,
> I have instant conductors all over me whether I pass
>   or stop.
> They seize every object and lead it harmlessly through me.
> I merely stir, press, feel with my fingers, and am happy.
> To touch my person to some one else's is about as much
>   as I can stand.[25]

To read Whitman is to feel alive, to be comfortable in one's skin and aware that the body is sheer gift and not to be feared. Here is a concluding stanza, grounded in Eden and touched by grace:

> As Adam early in the morning,
> walking forth from the bower refresh'd with sleep,
> behold me where I pass, hear my voice, approach.
> Touch me, touch the palm of your hand to my body as
>   I pass.
> Be not afraid of my body.[26]

Electricity and energy give way here to a deep calm and innocence, but Whitman is still speaking of the body. The eminent

American literary critic Harold Bloom relates how one summer, when he was undergoing a personal crisis, he began to read these lines of Whitman's poetry aloud as he sat with a friend fishing in Nantucket. After a while he was calmed and recovered himself again.[27]

The reference to recovery seems a good way to conclude this chapter. Christians have tended to forget that the word of God was also the word that spoke through nature, through flesh and blood, through the body of Jesus. Our history is littered with movements and sects that have perversely denied the bodily and emotional implications of the Incarnation and have sought to reduce Christianity 'to something lean and austere and cerebral . . . swinging the pendulum back from flesh to word'.[28] The work of recovery therefore continues: it is in dark, chaotic forces, in energy tamed and untamed, in emotions that elevate and distress, and bodies made for desire, delight and tenderness that the word made flesh can dwell and deeper truths about ourselves can be found.

8

Wisdom and silence: a testimony

————◦◆◦————

In this final chapter I want to begin with some verses from the book of Revelation that hold a continuing fascination for me:

> When the Lamb opened the seventh seal, there was silence in heaven for about half an hour. And I saw the seven angels who stand before God, and seven trumpets were given to them.
>
> Another angel with a golden censer came and stood at the altar; he was given a great quantity of incense to offer with the prayers of all the saints on the golden altar that is before the throne. (Rev. 8.1–3)

Why the fascination? The seventh seal is the final seal of the apocalyptic scroll containing the secret plan of judgement and salvation which cannot be revealed until the One who is worthy – the Lamb of God – breaks open the seal. The trumpet blasts of the angels herald desolation and destruction upon the earth, not unlike the plagues visited upon Egypt in the book of Exodus (7.14—10.23). The narrative is one of crisis before the End, interspersed with a period of silence that is part of the worship of the heavenly temple. According to Jewish tradition, at the time of the incense-offering the heavenly worshippers refrain from speech so that the prayers of those on earth can be heard in heaven.

The images are there to excite the imagination and still our chatter. They remind us of the importance of being silent as we presume to approach the presence of the All High. Not just in worship but also in the life of prayer and intercession, we begin to shrink when silence no longer informs that which we offer to God as our duty and delight. Mortal flesh should keep silence as we contemplate omnipotent love, or the 'true light which enlightens everyone' (John 1.9), and only ignorance or blindness can shield us from the abiding wisdom of the Psalms where we are ordered, 'Be still, and know that I am God' (46.10). It is in stillness, literally *stopping*, that we may come to know something of a hidden God, and of his disclosure in that which 'was from the beginning, what we have heard, what we have seen with our eyes, what we have looked at and touched with our hands, concerning the word of life' (1 John 1.1).

Something else of importance should also claim our attention here – the subtle intimation of a primeval silence. We are geared to thinking of beginnings in terms of the spacious and creative activity of God described in the opening of Genesis. Yet before the divine act of creation, or the Word that was there in the beginning with God (John 1.1), there was silence. Before there were stars to guide us or the night to cover us, there was neither noise nor speech – only the sound of silence in a 'formless void' (Genesis 1.2).

Earlier generations of believers understood this rather well. A famous painting by nineteenth-century artist Jean-François Millet depicts a farming couple praying the Angelus at dusk in the fields. They stand in an attitude of repose, tools set down and heads bowed in devotion, having heard the church bell in the distance. Before they take their evening rest they recall Mary, who consented to the angel's message, and Jesus her son, the fruit of her womb, who will come to renew the face of the earth with his brightness. The Angelus is the full stop that punctuates their days, momentarily eases their labours and forms in them the knowledge that beyond the work that provides their daily bread, there is the mystery and joy of the Incarnation and the 'gentle silence [that] enveloped all things' (Wisd. 18.14) in the beginning. It is not at all a sentimental picture and it is one I think of frequently as I toll my own church bell each morning and evening to signify a time of prayer to the parish. For me it captures something profound at the heart of Christian prayer and discipleship – that it is silence, not noise or busyness, that draws us closer to the deep, unifying realities of our lives and realigns the wayward heart and distracted mind in the direction of the kingdom of God.

The significance of silence for an authentic spiritual life is recognized and endorsed by all the great religions. The Hebrew word for the presence of God, *shekinah*, has the same root as the Arabic word *sukun* which describes the disciplined pause observed by devout Muslims as they pray five times each day. The Jew and the Muslim both understand how it is that in stillness God's truth and presence may be encountered. In Christianity those who made a special commitment to silence in the early centuries were called hesychasts, from the Greek word *hesychia* meaning quietness. Their sayings and teachings have been preserved and it is remarkable that for all their diversity and sometimes disarming eccentricity there is a common insistence that speech can often lead us astray and that without silence we are impoverished.[1] In the Hindu tradition they are designated *muni*, an ascription derived from a Sanskrit word which means 'to shut' – in this context, literally keeping one's mouth shut and not uttering a word. The instances are fairly rare but there are accounts of *muni* who kept silence for many years. In living under such a vow they come to recognize the emptiness of much speech, the vanity or need to impress that sometimes lies behind our words and the stupidity that often passes for conversation. Buddhism is particularly aware of the latter human tendency and depicts it as a serious obstacle to achieving enlightenment: 'They are so full of opinions on everything; and so they never come to know anything.'[2]

As a theological educator and writer with views and strong opinions on quite a lot of things, you will understand why I hesitated before including the previous quotation! Even in the first flush of teaching students, and occasionally after university days that seemed to have gone well, I recollect experiencing an inner emptiness on the way home – feeling that too much was said or attempted, that thoughts shared, however eloquent or sincere, somehow missed the point, that above all, a period of quietness would have brought a greater depth and wisdom to our deliberations. I had not been conspicuously shallow or silly but I was perhaps over-anxious to get from A to Z as comprehensively as possible in the time available. As time went on I came to know better, and to grasp that in all the great mysteries addressed by religion and philosophy we can only ever get from A to C interestingly and then leave the unanswered questions for another conversation! I also began to recognize in myself a deeper need for silence as a response to the mystery of things – a form of gratitude for the remarkable fact that anything exists at all and the sheer givenness of the world in all its complexity and fascination.

I desired to be silent before the mystery, and I travelled to find moments and places of stillness. Once, on a boat on the Sea of Galilee, as the engine was switched off and the pilgrims accompanying me fell quiet, we shared a collective remembrance of the dead calm brought about by the One who 'rebuked the winds and the sea' (Matt. 8.26) and urged his disciples to grow in faith and learn more about the life of a follower. On entering the great cathedral at Chartres for the first time, I was brought to my knees by the cavernous darkness, the brilliance of the stained glass, the altar that spoke of transcendence and the overarching quiet. Years later I came across these words of the twentieth-century French mystic and poet Charles Péguy, who on entering the same shrine had found a similar silence more eloquent than speech:

> Look at the piece of earth, all gathered and all quiet,
> Where silence, shadow and the ghostly reign,
> Where the eternal presence comes again,
> And soul finds that retreat, where it is itself once more.[3]

Early on one bright Ascension morning I slipped quietly into the chapel of the Order of the Holy Paraclete in Whitby. Much impressed me. The atmosphere seemed welcoming and expectant, but as the service progressed I was struck by the way in which the nuns recited the psalms. No fuss, no hurry and always a deliberate and audible pause in the middle of each sentence before continuing. Here was permission to breathe, think and imagine; space in which to allow a pause to become part of a wider, more disordered world beyond the liturgy; a full stop to bring order and perspective to the muddle and din that make up so much of the narrative of contemporary life. I had begun to learn this crucial lesson during my ministerial training but in the beauty of that Ascension morning my inner formation took a new turn. My wife and I made the decision to join the Order and live out its Rule in our daily lives.

Prayer and silence are woven into the fabric of each day. They help us to register what is happening in our lives and the lives of those who request our prayers and they stop us becoming careless when we presume to speak of God. In this way each day offers the possibility of what St Benedict calls the sanctifica-/ tion of the hours and the means of paying attention. 'Listen' is/ the first word of Benedict's Rule, and it is only in silence that the kind of listening he advocates is possible. Venerable monastic wisdom invites us to work and pray, but also to ground both in a silence that is neither passive nor empty and has the power to change us. Significantly, it is a form of wisdom that for many continues to prove attractive, even necessary – a gift from the past on which we can draw with each breath. We found evidence of this in unexpected places.

A few years ago Christine and I made an unusual pilgrimage together. As heavy snow began to fall and the force of nature made us feel puny by comparison, we drove thousands of miles, in cold and adverse conditions, through the beautiful emptiness of Canada, eventually arriving at the shrines of South Dakota on the Great Plains of America. We negotiated the Badlands with the respect they have accrued over centuries, noting the eeriness of silent trees that seemed to hold secrets never to be known. We took in the silence of the sacred Black Hills of the Lakota Indian tribe, and discovered the buffalo that had seemed destined to elude us as the afternoon grew dark and the weather more severe. We felt no rift between humanity and nature and had some sense of that continuity with other living things that Native Americans have always taken for granted.

At Wounded Knee on a grey, deserted Sunday afternoon we stood at the graves of the Indians who died in the massacre of 29 December 1890 when US military cannons cut down men, women and children alike. In less than an hour 150 Indians had been killed and 50 wounded, including Chief Big Foot, who was already gravely ill with pneumonia. Their crime had been to practise the Ghost Dance Religion,[4] which claimed that the earth would perish before coming alive again in a pure state to be inherited by the Indians in a world free from suffering. The Ghost Dance rituals included prayer, meditation and especially dancing, during which Indians might briefly experience a momentary vision of the paradise of green prairie grass and ample buffalo herds devoid of the presence of the white man, who had brought fear and terror. No one else was present that afternoon in the cemetery under a menacing sky. In the silence the scene of that original brutal and unnecessary violence felt uncommonly real and close.

At the memorial to the Oglala Lakota warrior Chief Crazy Horse, on the sacred ground of Thunderhead Mountain not far from Mount Rushmore, we steeled ourselves to see nothing of this great edifice, begun in 1948 and still far from completion. More than a million sightseers visit each year, but we had come on a morning of dense fog! The man on the entrance booth held out little prospect of success and even reduced the admission fee. It was our last day in America before travelling home and this site had played a large part in the planning of our trip. We paid up, went in, parked the car and stood gazing at the mountain, glad to be there but unsure what to do next. We said nothing, not even when the fog suddenly lifted to reveal the monument to the red man for whom the hills and earth bore the fingerprints of God.

In the silences of Dakota we found an experience of the holy. It is inhabited by few – on the surface, a barren place with harsh winters and little rain – but with its emptiness and huge skies there is a solitude that feeds the soul. The spirituality of the landscape stands comparison with the surroundings of the fourth-century monastics and teachers of wisdom who established themselves in the deserts of Egypt in order to free themselves from the chains of importance, noise and verbosity that can corrode the best intentions even when we are talking or teaching about spiritual matters. Dakota makes possible exposure – the awareness of inward contradictions and confusions and the need to make space for wider and more gracious visions. St Hilary, a fourth-century bishop (and also patron saint against snake bites and therefore a useful ally in the desert!) once noted, 'Everything that seems empty is full of the angels of God.' Those who live on the Plains seem to grasp this in the absence of traffic, the quietness of the sunrise, the sound of wind and birdsong, even the car coming from miles away. Dakota appears like a door into something more simple, but demanding – a cleansing of the perceptions and a spur to the prayerful thought that makes us more attuned to the world.

It is initially surprising (but then on reflection not at all) to learn that there are several monasteries on the Great Plains that keep silence at appointed hours and seek to find that elusive balance between the active and contemplative life. At the heart of their monasticism is the stillness, or stopping, I spoke of earlier, described by one community member as 'drawing water from an inexhaustible well'[5] – a powerful image that owes much to the wisdom and stories of the Bible. Each day in the relative emptiness of the Plains, the Scriptures are read and pondered; hospitality is given gladly to the stranger; essential chores and duties are performed; and in the deliberate quietness of life itself, with its recurring pattern of prayer, liturgy and silence, there emerges 'the madness of great love that sees God in all things'.[6] In *Conjectures of a Guilty Bystander*,[7] Thomas Merton writes about a trip to Louisville on an errand for his monastery. In the middle of a busy shopping mall he is suddenly overwhelmed by the realization that he loves all the people – that even though they are complete strangers, they are not alien to him.

This deep and compelling experience is more common than we suppose, tired and jaded as we often are in the presence of crowds. Merton's awareness of something unifying, tender and endearingly human clearly owes something to the empathy, curiosity and imagination that we encounter in writers and artists who are frequently struck by the pathos of the human condition that despite all our differences binds us together. As a proud Mancunian, I have always been drawn to the work of L. S. Lowry – a strange and idiosyncratic painter graced with a particular gift of looking at 'dirty old Northern towns' and finding in them what most of us miss most of the time: the extraordinary depths entailed in being human. He saw the world more vividly than others and immortalized the lives of the inconsequential – the nobodies making their way into the factories or enjoying precious moments of leisure, and the disabled who are often marginalized. Objecting to the sight of a cripple in one of Lowry's street scenes, a friend of his was taken by the artist on a tour of Manchester one afternoon. After just a few hours they counted 101 people with varying physical handicaps.

The same kind of sensibility is evident in Dickens, who spent hours walking the streets of London late at night, storing up his experiences and his reactions to them. Even in the Marylebone Workhouse, with its 2,000 residents including the newborn, infirm and dying, he was able to record instances of care and tenderness given to pauper children, who remained lively and cheerful in the presence of so many of society's rejects. And he was always engaged by those with whom he felt a particular emotional bond – the humble or lonely individuals who struggled to survive, who would never know success but were doing their best, sometimes in comic ways, to keep up appearances. In the Reading Room of the British Museum, he noticed a regular fellow reader, a man in a worn and threadbare suit. When a week or two passed and the man failed to appear, Dickens assumed that he had died but he was wrong. The man reappeared, this time in a bright black suit – a suit 'revived' by being painted over in glossy black paint. The effect was short-lived, as a rainy day completely removed the 'reviver'.[8] Dickens leaves the story there and offers no comment. But he writes out of the silence of the streets that he walked – the same silence experienced by Lowry as he went from house to house for 40 years collecting rents, living in shabby obscurity, and the solitude embraced by Merton that opened him up to the realization that there were no strangers, and the gate of heaven was everywhere.

What is it that unites the writer, the artist and the monk in this instance and constitutes a special approach to life? It has to do with their attitude to time and their ability to find and practise a particular and liberating constancy. In the middle of demands and duties they seem able to exercise a demanding form of recollection; and, in the case of Merton or the prayerful communities of the Great Plains, an embracing of the quiet but dominating rhythm of the daily liturgy that reveals the presence of the holy in unexpected places and makes sharper and clearer what is owed by way of compassion to the world. It is a form of commitment that enables silence, clarity and occasionally peace to be found within the clamour of the city as well as the desert.[9]

On a trip to Manhattan, an associate member of the Benedictines of Dakota found herself with a free evening as a result of a cancelled dinner date. She knew some Episcopalian nuns there, and phoned to ask them if she might share in the service of vespers and dinner. As the madness of a New York Friday night rush hour swirled around them, they sang plainsong, then ate a meal in silence. It was what she needed to bring a hectic week to a close, to recollect herself 'and even to experience a bit of that peace that passes understanding'.[10]

The scene she describes is familiar to me. It evokes good memories of visits to New York: celebrating the Eucharist for small religious communities while garbage trucks trundled noisily down the street collecting the trash; or one of the members of the Order, well into her eighties, preparing to carry heavy bags of food to the homeless in the neighbourhood. I recall keeping silence with nuns before the first service of the day, with their pet dog ambling into the chapel to join the gathering and as the noise of a restless city began to reassert itself. In the week leading up to Hallowe'en, I shared breakfast with them each morning in silence – just a nod or smile as orange juice was poured or bread toasted. Many of the shops nearby had made a special effort with their displays: magnificent pumpkins, flower arrays or spectacular ghouls in their windows to make the season fun as well as lucrative. The great cathedral of St John the Divine was showing a silent horror film from a previous era on a huge screen in the nave – a scary movie that still had the power to chill an eclectic congregation. The sisters took a different, more low-key approach, choosing to combine a holiday celebration with a touch of theology. Little witches perched on broomsticks could be seen by their breakfast plates; neither benevolent nor malign, they served as an amusing and pertinent reminder to guests that the sacred and profane are not easily separated. The unspoken text for the week was that God loves the whole of his creation and takes pleasure in creativity and imagination.

New York and Dakota continue to play an important part in my exploration and experience of silence and what it has to teach me. In their different ways, they represent wonderful and extraordinary places that open up new vistas and therefore the possibility of growth and change. Manhattan is filled with people and their stories: disappointment and confusion wrestle with hope and aspiration and its streets and avenues offer many opportunities for stillness and recollection. The Great Plains testify to a vivid continuum – all forms of life, animal and human, fused with 'Spirit' and occupying a good earth alive with quiet, transformative presences that we often find impossible even to imagine in our own restless and distracted culture.

Until I return, however, it is in the specific location of my life and ministry, not far from the great cities of Liverpool and Manchester and very close to a coastline of enveloping skies, spectacular sunsets and empty beaches, where time easily dissolves into something more spacious and a low tide can take the sea nearly two miles from shore, that I shall continue my pilgrimage.[11] There is no requirement to travel great distances in order to make silence our aim or learn more concerning its riches. Quite by chance, as I prepared these final thoughts, I found the following verse in a recent book, perhaps too easily and quickly discarded, nestling neglected in the corner of a luncheon club, almost hidden by a stack of historical romances and crime thrillers:

> To go to Rome
> Is much trouble, little profit.
> The King whom thou seekest there,
> Unless thou bring Him with thee, thou wilt not find.[12]

It is apparently a piece of old Celtic wisdom, suggesting that pilgrimage of itself is no guarantee of an encounter with God. Such work has to begin at home.

For me this is the chapel where each day I am confronted by the searching eye of Scripture and its precepts that are both liberating and costly. In stillness I can begin to ponder its gifts and demands. This is the place where intercession is offered in response to the poignant and sometimes distressing requests made on scribbled cards and hurried notes that represent what Wordsworth called 'the still, sad music of humanity'. Here too I try to honour the tentative hopes of those who dream of new beginnings, and seek to encourage them that the redemptive acts of God never cease. In this space, hallowed by the prayer and presence of generations before me, I am daily reminded that silence has been an integral part of the history of Christianity, and will remain so, if we continue to value what has been handed on to us.[13] For me this represents part of the necessary work of learning how I should be as a person – how I am to live faithfully and authentically in a world saturated by much that is unworthy of the human.

So I ring the bell. I light the candle before an icon of the Blessed Virgin, whose face reflects an impenetrable stillness that speaks to me. And, eventually, as I prepare to leave the chapel, I often say the words given to me by a priest long ago when I first offered myself for the ordained ministry: 'Lord, temper with tranquillity my manifold activity, that I may do my work for thee with very great simplicity.' Only after silence can I begin to pray such words with hope and integrity.

✓

Notes

1 What is wisdom?

1 The experience of those who feel cut off from the main events as they gaze at their computer screen is reflected in Edgar Allan Poe's prescient short story *The Man of the Crowd*, in which the narrator tracks an individual through the teeming streets of early Victorian London. As the day turns to night and the crowds disperse, the narrator realizes to his horror and surprise that the person he is following is pathologically terrified of solitude. He cannot be without a crowd or exist without it. He hurries on and on to the elusive location where he might discover himself 'among the dregs of the night town'. See Will Self, 'Madness of Crowds', *New Statesman*, 8 August 2011, p. 55.

2 See Ryszard Kapuscinski, *The Other* (London: Verso, 2008), p. 75. In these lectures Kapuscinski draws on the philosophy of Emmanuel Levinas, whose writings in the twentieth century confronted the crisis and atrophy of interpersonal relations in a mass society threatened by totalitarian systems. In the words of Professor Barbara Skarga, an expert on Levinas' philosophy, 'Levinas seeks to free us from the restraints of selfishness, from indifference, keep us from the temptation to be separate, to isolate ourselves and be withdrawn. He shows us a new dimension of the Self, namely that it is not just a solitary individual but that the composition of the Self also includes the Other' (p. 37).

3 R. J. Sternberg, ed., *Wisdom: Its Nature, Origins and Development* (Cambridge: Cambridge University Press, 1990).

4 Aristotle, *Nicomachean Ethics*, 1.2, trans. Terence Irwin (Indianapolis, IN: Hackett, 1985).

5 Significantly in this respect, the contemporary British philosopher Anthony Grayling has recently compiled a huge work drawing on the secular wisdom of many centuries. Arranged on the lines of the books of the Bible, it offers a humanist guide to living a good life. See his *The Good Book: A Secular Bible* (London: Bloomsbury, 2011). The publication of such a large and demanding text suggests that a secular culture is still willing to wrestle with matters of morals and meaning. Writing from a quite different perspective, Graham Ward

notes that even in an age frequently described as post-Christian, 'contemporary living is shot through with metaphysical themes, desires and dreams'. See his *The Politics of Discipleship: Becoming Post-Material Christians* (London: SCM Press, 2009), p. 152.

6 The American philosopher Susan Neiman has made an important contribution to this debate in her book *Moral Clarity: A Guide for Grown-Up Idealists* (Princeton, NJ: Princeton University Press, 2009).

7 Cited in Stephen S. Hall, *Wisdom: From Philosophy to Neuroscience* (London: Vintage Books, 2011), pp. 37–8.

8 The moral significance of distance, of how our intuitions support a stronger or weaker obligation to help those in need depending on how near or far they are in relation to us, is brought out in F. M. Kamm, *Intricate Ethics: Rights, Responsibilities and Permissible Harm* (Oxford: Oxford University Press, 2007), pp. 345–7.

9 Hall, *Wisdom*, p. 10.

10 Scripture sometimes makes the same clear distinction. The Wisdom of Solomon, for example, frequently portrays wisdom as the working of God but by contrast 'the reasoning of mortals is worthless, and our designs are likely to fail' (9.14).

11 The Four Noble Truths are represented by the following propositions:

Life means suffering.
The origin of suffering is attachment.
The cessation of suffering is attainable.
There is a path to the cessation of suffering.

12 For a fuller account of the journeys and the motivations that lay behind them see Felipe Fernandez-Armestos, *Truth: A History and a Guide for the Perplexed* (New York: Thomas Dunne, 1997), pp. 68–9.

13 Smith's obituary can be found in *The Economist*, 13 January 2011.

14 W. H. C. Frend provides an absorbing account of the differing and controversial interpretations of early Christianity in his *Saints and Sinners in the Early Church* (London: Darton, Longman and Todd, 1985).

15 Pius IX's 80 propositions, cited in his *Syllabus of Errors*, published 8 December 1864, are discussed in Garry Wills' *Papal Sin: Structures of Deceit* (New York: Doubleday, 2000), pp. 239–44.

16 George Weigel has noted of late 'an irrational and, let it be said frankly, deeply bigoted refusal to concede that Christian moral ideas have any place in the public square'. This phenomenon has been dubbed 'Christophobia' – a term coined by Joseph Weiler during the 2003 debates over the European Constitutional Treaty. See Weigel, 'Benedict XVI and the Future of the West', *Standpoint*, July/August 2011, p. 88.

17 The term 'mail carrier' is attributed to the Russian author Alexander Pushkin (1799–1837).

18 See Mahatma Gandhi, *The Essential Writings*, ed. Judith M. Brown (Oxford: Oxford World Classics, 2007), p. xii.

19 Hall, *Wisdom*, p. 13.

20 Some philosophers have sought to do this, reducing wisdom to a logical construct. See for example, Sharon Ryan, 'Humility Theory' in *The Stanford Encyclopedia of Philosophy* <www.plato.stanford.edu>.

21 Review of Stephen Hall's *Wisdom* by Ryan McIlhenny. See his 'Wisdom: That Stubborn Perversity' at <www.metanexus.net/magazine/tabid/68/id/10999/Default.aspx>.

2 The Hebrew Scriptures and the wisdom of Ecclesiastes

1 The author is identified by his pen-name Teacher, in Hebrew Qoheleth, probably meaning a 'gatherer' – one who is supposed to have accumulated wisdom and wealth with the authority to speak to an assembly or congregation. The unlikely identification with King Solomon (1.1) reflects 1 Kings 8.1 where Solomon preaches to the notables of Jerusalem. The date of the book is not settled, with scholars arguing for a date some time after 450 BC and no later than 200 BC.

2 Taken together, Proverbs, Job, Ecclesiastes, Sirach and the Wisdom of Solomon constitute a stream of Jewish biblical wisdom books concerned with knowledge and understanding and the frontier of the mysterious.

3 Part of a quotation from Pindar (Paean 7b), a Greek poet from the sixth century BC, cited in Bruno Snell, *Dichtung und Gesellschaft* (Hamburg: Claassen, 1965), p. 134.

4 Ben Witherington provides a comprehensive list of situational life topics in *Jesus the Sage: The Pilgrimage of Wisdom* (Edinburgh: T & T Clark, 1994), p. 83.

5 For a longer list of virtues see Anthony C. Thiselton, 'Wisdom in the Jewish and Christian Scriptures: The Hebrew Bible and Judaism', *Theology*, Vol. 114 No. 3, May/June 2011, pp. 167–8.

6 'The book of Proverbs can be read as among the earliest of self-help manuals. Its mantric code of prescribed behaviours – the serial, repetitious injunctions against lust, infidelity, imprudent business affairs, and similar pragmatic advice – is packaged as a wisdom instructional; the rhetorical style of its narrative establishes one of the iconic modes of transmission for Wisdom: father to son or, more generally, parent to child, elder to youth' (Stephen S. Hall, *Wisdom: From Philosophy to Neuroscience*, London: Vintage Books, 2011, p. 3).

7 Gerhard von Rad, *Wisdom in Israel* (London: SCM Press, 1972), p. 102.

8 Søren Kierkegaard (1813–55), extract from his *Edifying Discourses*.

9 Thiselton, 'Wisdom in the Jewish and Christian Scriptures', p. 172.

10 Von Rad notes in *Wisdom in Israel*: 'As opposed to the exclusiveness of her religious convictions, Israel was not only aware of the search for knowledge on the part of other nations, but also studied its products and was not above appropriating from it what seemed to be useful' (p. 38).

11 Paul Ricoeur, 'Towards a Hermeneutic of the Idea of Revelation', *Essays on Biblical Interpretation* (London: SPCK, 1981), pp. 85–6.

12 Hall, *Wisdom*, p. 13.

13 Thiselton, 'Wisdom in the Jewish and Christian Scriptures', p. 13.

14 Anton Schoors, 'Theodicy in Qohelet', in Antti Laato and Johannes C. de Moor (eds), *Theodicy in the World of the Bible* (Leiden: Brill, 2003), p. 376.

15 Harold Bloom, *Where Shall Wisdom be Found?* (New York: Riverhead Books, 2004), p. 28.

16 Von Rad, *Wisdom in Israel*, p. 233.

17 Colin Wilson, *Beyond the Outsider* (London: Pan, 1972), p. 29.

18 Rainer Maria Rilke, Bohemian-Austrian poet (1875–1929). This is the first line of his best-known work, *Duino Elegies*.

19 John Updike, *Due Considerations: Essays and Criticism* (London: Hamish Hamilton, 2007), pp. 40–1.

20 Ralph Waldo Emerson (1803–82), American poet and essayist.

21 Patti Smith, *Just Kids* (New York: HarperCollins, 2010), cited in Stephanie Paulsell, 'Into the Infinite Together', *Harvard Divinity Bulletin*, Winter/Spring 2012, p. 69.

22 William James (1842–1910) was the brother of novelist Henry James and famous for his monumental *Principles of Psychology* (1890), which runs to 1,200 pages, and his account of *The Varieties of Religious Experience* (1902).

23 'Qoheleth's monologue is presented as the monologue of a wise man reflecting on his experience, but the book seems suspicious of such claims to wisdom; self-contradiction therefore is embedded at its deepest level' (Stuart Weeks, 'Commentary on Ecclesiastes', in John Barton and John Muddiman (eds), *The Oxford Bible Commentary*, Oxford: Oxford University Press, 2000, p. 423).

24 <www.philosophicalsociety.com/Archives/The%20Healthy-Minded%20&%20Sick%20Soul.htm>, p. 6.

25 <www.philosophicalsociety.com/Archives/The%20Healthy-Minded%
20&%20Sick%20Soul.htm>, p. 10.

26 <www.philosophicalsociety.com/Archives/The%20Healthy-Minded%
20&%20Sick%20Soul.htm>, p. 3.

27 A passage from Kierkegaard's novel *Repetition* (1843).

28 'We do not know where or how it took place. As in a gradual morning
light, prehistoric hominids must have come to regard, to identify themselves as other than animals. Or, in a revolution of consciousness,
far greater than any since, as being animals of a special breed'. George
Steiner, writer and literary critic, commenting on the emergence of
human consciousness in *My Unwritten Books* (London: Weidenfeld
and Nicolson, 2008), p. 154.

29 Quotation from Marilynne Robinson, *When I Was a Child I Read Books*
(London: Virago, 2012), p. 185. See in particular her chapter 'Cosmology'
(pp. 182–202) for an important overview of the place of humanity
in the cosmos from the perspective of science and religion.

30 'It has been the "God-question", that of God's existence or non-
existence, and the attempts to give to this existence "a habitation
and a name", which until very recently have fuelled much of great
art, literature and speculative constructs. They have provided consciousness with its centre of gravity' (Steiner, *My Unwritten Books*,
p. 191).

31 Rowan Williams, *Resurrection* (London: Darton, Longman and Todd,
1982), p. 41.

32 Jessica Martin explores the tension between the vision of Ecclesiastes
and the Christian hope in 'Mortality and its Joys: Reading Ecclesiastes
in the light of the Gospel Resurrection Narratives', *Theology*, Vol. 111
No. 864, November/December 2008, pp. 442–9.

3 The wisdom of the Incarnation: the prologue of St John's Gospel

1 M. W. G. Stibbe, *John* (Sheffield: JSOT Press, 1993), pp. 22–3.

2 T. W. Manson, *Bulletin of the John Rylands Library*, Vol. 30 No. 2,
May 1947, p. 320 n.1.

3 Some notable commentators have argued that the prologue was
composed quite independently of the Fourth Gospel by a writer
belonging to a Hellenistic Jewish background. See for example R. E.
Brown, *The Gospel According to John I–XII* (New York: Doubleday,
1966), pp. 18–23.

4 Walt Whitman (1819–92), American poet, essayist and journalist.

5 Much later in the Gospel he writes, 'these are written so that you may come to believe that Jesus is the Messiah, the Son of God, and that through believing you may have life in his name' (John 20.31).

6 Cornelius Ernst, *Multiple Echo: Explorations in Theology*, ed. Fergus Kerr and Timothy Radcliffe (London: Darton, Longman and Todd, 1979), p. 85.

7 Neil Richardson, *John for Today: Reading the Fourth Gospel* (London: SCM Press, 2010), p. 5.

8 James Jones, *With My Whole Heart* (London: SPCK, 2012), p. 100.

9 *The Observer*, 5 August 2012.

10 During a stay in England in 1817, Poe was registered at the Reverend John Bransby's Manor House School at Stoke Newington, then a suburb four miles north of London.

11 Alister E. McGrath, *Christian Theology: An Introduction* (Oxford: Blackwell, 1994), p. 288.

12 Geza Vermes, *Christian Beginnings: From Nazareth to Nicaea AD 30–325* (London: Allen Lane, 2012) p. 133.

13 Philo, *On the Confusion of Tongues*, 11.146–7.

14 Philo, *Abraham*, 1.121, trans. F. H. Colson and G. H. Whitaker (Loeb Classical Library, 1929).

15 Karen Armstrong, *The Bible: The Biography* (London: Atlantic Books, 2007), p. 53.

16 Philo, *The Migration of Abraham*, 11.34–5.

17 Irenaeus, *Against Heresies*, 4:23.

18 Augustine, *Confessions*, VII.9, trans. R. S. Pine-Coffin (London: Penguin, 1961), pp. 144–5.

19 The term is associated with a former Archbishop of Canterbury, Michael Ramsey, who in his writings memorably affirmed that 'God is Christ-like and in him is no unChristlikeness at all.'

20 R. H. Lightfoot, *St John's Gospel: A Commentary* (Oxford: Oxford University Press, 1956), p. 50.

21 See Owen Chadwick, *Michael Ramsey: A Life* (London: SCM Press, 1990), p. 39.

22 Chadwick, *Michael Ramsey*, p. 41.

23 Chadwick, *Michael Ramsey*, p. 41.

24 Chadwick, *Michael Ramsey*, p. 46.

25 Chadwick, *Michael Ramsey*, p. 46.

26 A. M. Ramsey, *The Glory of God and the Transfiguration of Christ* (London: Longmans, 1949), p. 151.

27 R. E. C. Browne, *Love of the World: Collected Papers*, ed. Ian Corbett (Worthing: Churchman Publishing, 1986), p. 42.

28 'Ramsey, Canterbury Pilgrim' (1974), cited in Douglas Dales, John Habgood, Geoffrey Rowell and Rowan Williams (eds), *Glory Descending: Michael Ramsey and His Writings* (London: Canterbury Press, 2005) p. 16.

29 Along with John 1.18; 20.28 and Romans 9.5, this verse is one of the rare places in the New Testament where Christ may be referred to as God.

30 See the hymn 'Behold, the great Creator makes' (*New English Hymnal*).

31 Taken from J. H. Newman, 'An Essay on Poetry' (1829), cited by A. Ecclestone, *Yes to God* (London: Darton, Longman and Todd, 1975), p. 59.

32 *Les Vraies Richesses* by Jean Giono, cited by H. de Lubac in *Catholicism* (English translation, London: Burns and Oates, 1950).

33 Johann Wolfgang von Goethe (1749–1832), German writer, artist, poet, diplomat and philosopher. The quotation is taken from *Poems of West and East* (1819).

4 The wisdom of St Paul

1 A. N. Wilson, *Paul: The Mind of the Apostle* (London: Sinclair-Stevenson, 1997), p. 84.

2 Gaius Cornelius Tacitus (AD 56–117), senator and a historian of the Roman Empire. This extract is cited from *Annals*, 15.44.2, 4.

3 Anthony Trollope (1815–82), English author of 47 novels and 16 books in other genres.

4 After James's seminal work on this subject, the other classic text is *Mysticism* (1911) by Evelyn Underhill (1815–1941). Underhill was an English Anglo-Catholic writer and pacifist who wrote extensively on religious and spiritual practices. *Mysticism* is her best-known work and it represents her study 'of the nature and development of man's spiritual consciousness'. She was unimpressed by some aspects of James's earlier work, finding it too scientific and objective. Where she struck new ground was in her insistence that divine union produced a glorious and fruitful creativeness: 'for the mystics winter is over . . . life, new, unquenchable and lovely comes to meet them with the dawn' (p. 47).

5 Paul uses the third person here but it seems clear that he is referring to himself.

6 The phrase is attributed to Mircea Eliade, the notable twentieth-century scholar of comparative religions.

7 Adolf Gustav Deissman, *Paul: A Study in Social and Religious History* (New York: Harper & Row, 1957), pp. 88, 140.

8 Neil Richardson, *Paul for Today: New Perspectives on a Controversial Apostle* (London: Epworth, 2008), p. 91.

9 David Tracy, in *God, Jesus and the Spirit*, ed. D. Callahan (New York: Herder, 1969), p. 328.

10 Augustine, *Confessions*, X.6, trans. R. S. Pine-Coffin (London: Penguin, 1961), p. 211.

11 Adrian Hastings, *The Theology of a Protestant Catholic* (London: SCM Press, 1990), p. 170.

12 Paul, who writes that man is the head of the woman and that women should be silent in church, also speaks in his epistles of a number of women as if they are leaders of Christian gatherings. In Romans 16.1–2 he writes, 'I commend to you our sister Phoebe, a deacon of the church at Cenchreae', applying to her the Greek word *diakonos* that he applies to himself and Timothy. He also writes: 'Husbands, love your wives' (Col. 3.19); and, 'There is no longer Jew or Greek, there is no longer slave or free, there is no longer male and female; for all of you are one in Christ Jesus' (Gal. 3.28).

13 George Herbert (1593–1633), Welsh-born poet, orator and Anglican priest of a small parish near Salisbury, where he cared unfailingly for his parishioners and was described as 'a most glorious saint and seer'.

14 J. Hollingdale, *A Nietzsche Reader* (London: Penguin, 1977), p. 20. In a similar vein Nietzsche also wrote, in *Thus Spake Zarathustra* (1883–85), 'One must also have chaos in oneself in order to give birth to a dancing star' (1.v). The work deals with the famous parable on 'the death of God' and the prophecy of the *Ubermensch*, or Superman.

5 Wisdom and the ethics of reading

1 The dear friend and fellow worker is Timothy, and Troas is ancient Troy, the departure point from Asia to Europe (see 2 Tim. 4.13). The letter 2 Timothy purports to be from Paul but some scholars, without denying its authenticity, argue that the epistle contains some later teaching along with genuine fragments of Paul. See James D. Miller, *The Pastoral Letters as Composite Documents* (two vols, Cambridge: Cambridge University Press, 1997).

2 N. T. Wright, 'Israel's Scriptures in Paul's Narrative Theology', *Theology*, Vol. 115 No. 5, September/October 2012, p. 325.

3 I first came across this interesting term in the work of the writer Alberto Manguel, born in Buenos Aires, raised in Israel, a Canadian

citizen and currently resident in France. He is the author of dozens of books, the editor of anthologies and the owner of a personal library that runs to thousands of volumes on a diverse range of subjects.

4 From the celebrated 'To be, or not to be' soliloquy in Shakespeare's *Hamlet* (1602).

5 Quoted in Alan Jacobs, *The Pleasures of Reading in an Age of Distraction* (Oxford: Oxford University Press, 2011). In a similar vein, the accomplished novelist Zadie Smith confessed in a recent interview that she was making use of a special app to deny her access to the internet when she was trying to write!

6 Even Augustine, with far fewer books at his disposal, is worried by how his colleagues will find time to apply themselves to study: 'But where shall truth be sought or when? Ambrose has no leisure; we have no leisure to read; where shall we find even the books?' (E. B. Pusey, *Confessions of St Augustine*, London: Thomas Nelson and Sons, 1938, pp. 123–4). The Ambrose in question is St Ambrose, Bishop of Milan and Doctor of the Church (died 397).

7 The young Copperfield read voraciously, particularly popular adventure novels, some of which, including Cervantes' *Don Quixote*, are now considered classics.

8 Attributed to the eighteenth-century scientist G. C. Lichtenberg.

9 The *Oxford English Dictionary* records that older meanings of 'studio' became obsolete after 1697.

10 From the Latin expression *per ardua ad astra*.

11 Alberto Manguel, *A Reader on Reading* (New Haven, CT: Yale University Press 2010), p. 162. Commenting further on the importance of reading slowly, Manguel relates that when Vladimir Nabokov was teaching his students how to read Kafka, he pointed out to them that the insect into which Gregor Samsa is transformed is a winged beetle, an insect that carries wings under its armoured back. If Gregor had only discovered them, he would have been able to escape. Nabokov then added: 'Many a Dick and Jane grow up like Gregor, unaware that they too have wings and can fly' (p. 160).

12 Manguel, *A Reader on Reading*, p. 189.

13 Alan Jacobs has good and useful things to say on this matter in *The Pleasures of Reading*.

14 Jacobs, *The Pleasures of Reading*, p. 89, quoting a passage from the memoir of Lynne Sharon Schwartz, *Ruined by Reading* (Boston, MA: Beacon Press, 1996).

15 Quotation from the poet laureate Carol Ann Duffy in an interview in *The Times*, 1 October 2011.

6 Wisdom and music

1 Karen Armstrong, *The Spiral Staircase* (New York: Alfred A. Knopf, 2004), p. 10.
2 Pablo Casals, *Joys and Sorrows* (London: Macdonald, 1970).
3 The person in question is Michael Steinberg, formerly music critic of the *Boston Globe*. Michael Steinberg and Larry Rothe, *For the Love of Music* (Oxford: Oxford University Press, 2006), p. 24.
4 Steinberg and Rothe, *For the Love of Music*, p. 167.
5 Canadian rock musician Neil Young, cited in 'Ragged Glory', a review of his album *Psychedelic Pill* in *New Statesman*, 16–22 November 2012.
6 James Lancelot, 'Music as a Sacrament', in David Brown and Ann Loades (eds), *The Sense of the Sacramental* (London: SPCK, 1995), p. 183.
7 Imogen Holst, *Bach* (London: Faber and Faber, 1965), p. 60.
8 Holst, *Bach*, p. 45.
9 Barely halfway through his life he composed *Come, Thou Lovely Hour of Dying*, a simple, flowing tune for recorders, early evidence of Bach's tranquil attitude to death.
10 On passing through Leipzig in 1789, Mozart heard a choir rehearsing Bach's eight-part motet *Sing to the Lord*. When the singing was finished, he exclaimed, 'Here is something one can learn from' (Holst, *Bach*, p. 87).
11 The phrase is from *Paradise Lost*, Book 2, 147–8.
12 From the sixth movement of *The Song of the Earth*.
13 Letter to Arnold Berliner, in Gustav Mahler, *Selected Letters*, ed. Knud Martner, Eithne Wilkins and Ernest Kaiser, trans. Bill Hopkins (London: Faber and Faber, 1979), p. 127.
14 Cited by Norman Lebrecht, *Why Mahler? How One Man and Ten Symphonies Changed the World* (London: Faber and Faber, 2010), p. 76.
15 Lebrecht, *Why Mahler?*, pp. 75–6.
16 From 'I am lost to the world', one of the five songs by the poet Friedrich Rückert that Mahler set to music.
17 Roger Scruton, *The Face of God* (London: Continuum, 2012) p. 169.
18 Scruton, *The Face of God*, p. 172.
19 These are, as I explained, personal choices. For a fascinating broader survey of the musical cultures of the twentieth century and their earlier influences, see Alex Ross, *The Rest is Noise: Listening to the Twentieth Century* (London: Fourth Estate, 2008).

20 Steinberg and Rothe, *For the Love of Music*, p. 240.

21 A quotation from President Abraham Lincoln's First Inaugural Address, 4 March 1861.

7 Wisdom and the emotions

1 Janet Morley, *All Desires Known* (London: Movement for the Ordination of Women, 1988), p. 5.

2 'Breathe through the heats of our desire, thy coolness and thy balm', from the concluding verse of 'Dear Lord and Father of Mankind', regularly voted as one of the nation's favourite hymns.

3 One common definition of a parable states that it is 'a brief, succinct story, in prose or verse that illustrates a moral or religious lesson . . . and generally features human characters'. See John Dominic Crossan, *The Power of Parable: How Fiction by Jesus became Fiction about Jesus* (London: SPCK, 2012), p. 30.

4 M. F. Meyer, 'That Whale among the Fishes: The Theory of Emotions', *Psychological Review*, Vol. 40, 1933, p. 300.

5 Augustine, *Confessions*, X.28, trans. R. S. Pine-Coffin (London: Penguin, 1961), p. 232.

6 Martha C. Nussbaum, *Upheavals of Thought: The Intelligence of Emotions* (Cambridge: Cambridge University Press, 2001), p. 19.

7 Nussbaum, *Upheavals of Thought*, p. 21.

8 Seneca (4 BC–AD 65), Roman Stoic, philosopher, statesman and dramatist. A tutor and adviser to the emperor Nero, he was later forced to commit suicide because of his alleged complicity in a conspiracy.

9 'Feigning total certainty: we all do it, all the time. Parents have to seem certain to children, teachers to pupils, doctors to patients. We're suspicious of uncertainty, of the murky territory of doubt. We want to be coddled in that grid system where everything is numbered and ordered, where we know exactly, where we stand all the time' (Sophie Elmhirst, 'There's a Freedom in Losing Your Bearings', *New Statesman*, 14–20 December 2012, p. 62).

10 Thomas Hobbes, *Leviathan* (1651).

11 Michael McGhee, *Transformations of Mind: Philosophy as Spiritual Practice* (Cambridge: Cambridge University Press, 2000), p. 47.

12 McGhee, *Transformations of Mind*, p. 48.

13 McGhee, *Transformations of Mind*, p. 48.

14 McGhee, *Transformations of Mind*, p. 48.

15 Paraphrase of final lines of 'To His Coy Mistress' by Andrew Marvell (1621–78).

16 McGhee, *Transformations of Mind*, p. 56.

17 McGhee, *Transformations of Mind*, p. 56.

18 I owe the recollection of this story and its precepts to Jeanette Winterson in her memoir, *Why Be Happy When You Could Be Normal?* (London: Vintage Books, 2012), pp. 34–5.

19 A phrase I've borrowed and adapted from Nietzsche's *Twilight of the Idols* (1889).

20 Frances Ashcroft, *The Spark of Life: Electricity in the Human Body* (London: Allen Lane, 2012), p. 257.

21 A few years after the end of the Civil War in 1865, Whitman wrote: 'Future years will never know the seething hell and the black infernal background of countless minor scenes and interiors (not the few great battles) of the Secession War; and it is best they should not. In the mushy influences of current times, the fervid atmosphere and typical events of those years are in danger of being totally forgotten . . . Its interior history will not only never be written, its practicality, minutiae of deeds and passions, will never be even suggested' (*Memoranda During the War*).

22 Excerpt from notebook drafts cited in Harold Bloom, *The Western Canon: The Books and School of the Ages* (New York: Macmillan, 1995), p. 276.

23 In his thinking here Whitman is close to the early and complex Christian notion of *theosis* – 'of God becoming man, in order that man might become God'. The teaching finds support in Scripture (Ps. 82.6; 2 Pet. 1.4), and was promulgated by theologians of the eminence of Irenaeus and Athanasius. Interestingly, from a non-Christian perspective, even modern writers find astonishing our capacity to transcend human limitations and become God-like in our seeing and understanding. Writing about the Higgs boson particle discovered in the Large Hadron Collider at CERN (the European Organization for Nuclear Research) in 2012, the scientist Brian Cox comments: 'How astonishing it is that a small group of apes on an insignificant rock among hundreds of billions in the Milky Way galaxy were able to predict the existence of a piece of nature that condensed into the vacuum of space less than a billionth of a second after the universe began 13.75 billion years ago' ('The Coldest Place in the Universe', *New Statesman*, 21 December 2012–3 January 2013, pp. 26–8).

24 'I sing the body electric': stanza 19 in Whitman's *Leaves of Grass* (first published 1855).

25 'Song of Myself', a poem of 52 stanzas that established itself as 'the American epic that defines the ethos of the nation', quoted in Harold

Bloom, *The Best Poems of the English Language* (New York: Harper Perennial, 2007), p. 531.

26 'As Adam early in the morning', the conclusion of 'Song of Myself'.

27 Bloom, *The Western Canon*, p. 289.

28 John Habgood, *Faith and Uncertainty* (London: Darton, Longman and Todd, 1997), p. 68.

8 Wisdom and silence: a testimony

1 See John Chryssavgis, *In the Heart of the Desert: The Spirituality of the Desert Fathers and Mothers* (Bloomington, IN: World Wisdom Books, 2003).

2 Donald Nicholl, *Holiness* (Darton, Longman and Todd, 1981), p. 69.

3 Cited in Alan Ecclestone, *A Staircase for Silence* (London: Darton, Longman and Todd, 1977), p. 38.

4 Introduced across the American West in 1888 by Paiute holy man Wovoka from Nevada, son of the mystic Tavibo.

5 Kathleen Norris, *Dakota: A Spiritual Geography* (New York: Houghton Mifflin, 1993), p. 183.

6 Norris, *Dakota*, p. 16.

7 Published in New York by Doubleday, 1966. Merton was a Trappist monk and author of many books on the spiritual life that had to be lived in the conflicts and turmoil of mid-twentieth-century America.

8 Claire Tomalin records this touching incident in *Charles Dickens: A Life* (London: Penguin Viking, 2011), p. 41.

9 Robert A. Ferguson explores American literature's encounters with solitude with particular reference to the country's openness, mobility, spaciousness and flux in *Alone in America: The Stories that Matter* (Cambridge, MA: Harvard University Press, 2013).

10 Norris, *Dakota*, p. 17.

11 The award-winning poet Jean Sprackland has recently published an account of a year spent exploring the coastline between Formby and Southport: *Strands: A Year of Discoveries on the Beach* (London: Jonathan Cape, 2012).

12 From *The Irish Liber Hymnorum* (Henry Bradshaw Society, 1898), cited in Maggi Dawn, *The Accidental Pilgrim: New Journeys on Ancient Pathways* (London: Hodder and Stoughton, 2011), p. 145.

13 Diarmaid MacCulloch has recently addressed this theme in the 2011/12 Gifford Lectures, 'Silence in Christian History', now published in book form as *Silence: A Christian History* (London: Allen Lane, 2013).

Select bibliography

Aristotle (1985) *Nicomachean Ethics*, trans. T. Irwin. Indianapolis, IN: Hackett.

Armstrong, K. (2007) *The Bible: The Biography*. London: Atlantic Books.

Ashcroft, F. (2012) *The Spark of Life: Electricity in the Human Body*. London: Allen Lane.

Augustine (1961) *Confessions*, trans. R. S. Pine-Coffin. London: Penguin.

Bloom, H. (1995) *The Western Canon: The Books and School of the Ages*. New York: Macmillan.

Bloom, H. (2004) *Where Shall Wisdom be Found?* New York: Riverhead Books.

Bloom, H. (2007) *The Best Poems of the English Language*. New York: Harper Perennial.

Brown, D. and Loades, A. (1995) *The Sense of the Sacramental*. London: SPCK.

Brown, R. E. (1966), *The Gospel According to John I–XII*. New York: Doubleday.

Browne, R. E. C. (1986), in I. Corbett (ed.), *Love of the World: Collected Papers*. Worthing: Churchman Publishing.

Callahan, D. (ed.) (1969) *God, Jesus and the Spirit*. New York: Herder.

Casals, P. (1970) *Joys and Sorrows*. London: Macdonald.

Chadwick, O. (1990) *Michael Ramsey: A Life*. London: SCM Press.

Chryssavgis, J. (2003) *In the Heart of the Desert: The Spirituality of the Desert Fathers and Mothers*. Bloomington, IN: World Wisdom Books.

Crossan, J. D. (2012) *The Power of Parable: How Fiction by Jesus became Fiction about Jesus*. London: SPCK.

Dawn, M. (2011) *The Accidental Pilgrim: New Journeys on Ancient Pathways*. London: Hodder & Stoughton.

Deissman, A. G. (1957) *Paul: A Study in Religious and Social History*. New York: Harper & Row.

Ecclestone, A. (1975) *Yes to God*. London: Darton, Longman and Todd.

Ecclestone, A. (1977) *A Staircase for Silence*. London: Darton, Longman and Todd.

Ernst, C. (1979), in F. Kerr and T. Radcliffe (eds), *Multiple Echo: Explorations in Theology*. London: Darton, Longman and Todd.

Ferguson, R. A. (2013) *Alone in America: The Stories that Matter.* Cambridge, MA: Harvard University Press.

Fernandez-Armestos, F. (1997) *Truth: A History and a Guide for the Perplexed.* New York: Thomas Dunne.

Frend, W. H. C. (1985) *Saints and Sinners in the Early Church.* London: Darton, Longman and Todd.

Gandhi, M. (2007) *The Essential Writings,* ed. J. M. Brown. Oxford: Oxford World Classics.

Grayling, A. C. (2011) *The Good Book: A Secular Bible.* London: Bloomsbury.

Habgood, J. (1997) *Faith and Uncertainty.* London: Darton, Longman and Todd.

Hall, S. (2011) *Wisdom: From Philosophy to Neuroscience.* London: Vintage Books.

Hastings, A. (1990) *The Theology of a Protestant Catholic.* London: SCM Press.

Hollingdale, J. (1977) *A Nietzsche Reader.* London: Penguin.

Holst, I. (1965) *Bach.* London: Faber and Faber.

Jacobs, A. (2011) *The Pleasures of Reading in an Age of Distraction.* London: Oxford University Press.

Jones, J. (2012) *With My Whole Heart.* London: SPCK.

Kamm, F. M. (2007) *Intricate Ethics: Rights, Responsibilities and Permissible Harm.* Oxford: Oxford University Press.

Kapuscinski, R. (2008) *The Other.* London: Verso.

Lebrecht, N. (2010) *Why Mahler? How One Man and Ten Symphonies Changed the World.* London: Faber and Faber.

Lightfoot, R. H. (1956) *St John's Gospel: A Commentary.* Oxford: Oxford University Press.

McGhee, M. (2000) *Transformations of Mind: Philosophy as Spiritual Practice.* Cambridge: Cambridge University Press.

McGrath, A. E. (1994) *Christian Theology: An Introduction.* Oxford: Blackwell.

Manguel, A. (2010) *A Reader on Reading.* New Haven, CT: Yale University Press.

Miller, J. D. (1997) *The Pastoral Letters as Composite Documents.* 2 vols, Cambridge: Cambridge University Press.

Morley, J. (1988) *All Desires Known.* London: Movement for the Ordination of Women.

Neiman, S. (2009) *Moral Clarity: A Guide for Grown-Up Idealists.* Princeton, NJ: Princeton University Press.

Nicholl, D. (1981) *Holiness.* London: Darton, Longman and Todd.

Norris, K. (1993) *Dakota: A Spiritual Geography*. New York: Houghton Mifflin.

Nussbaum, M. (2001) *Upheavals of Thought: The Intelligence of Emotions*. Cambridge: Cambridge University Press.

Ramsey, A. M. (1949) *The Glory of God and the Transfiguration of Christ*. London. Longmans.

Richardson, N. (2008) *Paul for Today: New Perspectives on a Controversial Apostle*. London: Epworth.

Richardson, N. (2010) *John for Today: Reading the Fourth Gospel*. London: SCM Press.

Ricoeur, P. (1981) *Essays on Biblical Interpretation*. London: SPCK.

Robinson, M. (2012) *When I Was a Child I Read Books*. London: Virago.

Ross, A. (2008) *The Rest is Noise: Listening to the Twentieth Century*. London: Fourth Estate.

Scruton, R. (2012) *The Face of God*. London: Continuum.

Smith, P. (2010) *Just Kids*. New York: HarperCollins.

Sprackland, J. (2012) *Strands: A Year of Discoveries on the Beach*. London: Jonathan Cape.

Steinberg, M. and Rothe, L. (2006) *For the Love of Music*. Oxford: Oxford University Press.

Steiner, G. (2008) *My Unwritten Books*. London: Weidenfeld & Nicolson.

Stibbe, M. W. G. (1993) *John*. Sheffield: JSOT Press.

Tomalin, C. (2011) *Charles Dickens: A Life*. London: Penguin Viking.

Updike, J. (2007) *Due Considerations: Essays and Criticism*. London: Hamish Hamilton.

Vermes, G. (2012) *Christian Beginnings: From Nazareth to Nicaea AD 30–325*. London: Allen Lane.

Von Rad, G. (1972) *Wisdom in Israel*. London: SCM Press.

Ward, G. (2009) *The Politics of Discipleship: Becoming Post-Material Christians*. London: SCM Press.

Williams, R. (1982) *Resurrection*. London: Darton, Longman and Todd.

Wills, G. (2000) *Papal Sin: Structures of Deceit*. New York: Doubleday.

Wilson, A. N. (1997) *Paul: The Mind of the Apostle*. London: Sinclair-Stevenson.

Wilson, C. (1972) *Beyond the Outsider*. London: Pan.

Winterson, J. (2012) *Why Be Happy When You Could Be Normal?* London: Vintage Books.

Witherington, B. (1994) *Jesus the Sage: The Pilgrimage of Wisdom*. Edinburgh: T. & T. Clark.